DIY YouTube
Channel
by STEM SCHOOL

DIY YouTube Channel

Build, Grow & Monetize Your DIY Tech Channel

By

STEM School

This Page Left Intentionally Blank

Contents

Chapter 1

Introduction to Tech YouTube Channels

In the modern digital age, YouTube has become one of the most powerful platforms for sharing knowledge, entertainment, and information. Among the vast array of content available on YouTube, tech-focused channels have seen a dramatic rise in both popularity and influence. The increasing complexity and innovation in technology have created a high demand for content that simplifies, explains, and showcases these advancements. This chapter explores the concept of a YouTube channel focused on tech content, why this niche is growing rapidly, and the key benefits of starting a tech-based YouTube channel. It also outlines the mindset, skills, and tools required to succeed in the tech niche, laying a solid foundation for building and growing a successful channel.

The Rise of Tech YouTube Channels

Technology is deeply integrated into everyday life, influencing how people work, communicate, and entertain themselves. From the rise of smartphones and smart home devices to the increasing interest in artificial intelligence, robotics, and automation, there is a growing need for content that helps users understand and leverage these advancements.

The popularity of tech-based YouTube channels can be attributed to several key factors-

Complexity of Technology- As technology becomes more complex, the average user seeks simple explanations and practical demonstrations. YouTube provides a visual and interactive platform for breaking down complex topics into easy-to-understand content.

Consumer Decisions- With the rapid pace of technological innovation, consumers are constantly looking for guidance on purchasing decisions. Tech review channels, unboxing videos, and comparison tests help viewers make informed choices.

Hands-On Learning- Many viewers prefer learning through direct, hands-on experience rather than reading text-based guides. DIY tech channels that demonstrate projects, repairs, and modifications have become highly valuable resources.

Tech Enthusiast Communities- Tech YouTube channels often create communities of like-minded individuals who share their passion for technology. Viewers engage through comments, discussions, and shared experiences, building a sense of belonging.

Monetization Potential- The tech niche tends to attract a higher CPM (cost per thousand impressions) due to the value of the target audience. Advertisers are willing to pay more to reach a tech-savvy demographic, making tech channels particularly profitable.

To understand why tech-based content has become so influential, it's important to examine the growth of YouTube itself.

Growth of YouTube and Tech Content

YouTube, launched in 2005, quickly evolved from a simple video-sharing site into the second-largest search engine in the world (after Google). The following table provides key data on YouTube's growth and the increasing dominance of tech content-

Year	Total Active Users (Billions)	Daily Video Views (Billions)	Percentage of Tech Content Views (%)	Top Tech Channel Subscribers (Millions)
2010	0.8	2	8	5
2015	1.5	5	12	15
2020	2.3	10	18	35
2025*	3.0 (projected)	15 (projected)	22 (projected)	50+ (projected)

*Projected based on current growth trends.

The table demonstrates that both YouTube usage and the consumption of tech content have grown significantly over the years. Tech content represents one of the fastest-growing categories on the platform due to the increasing relevance of technology in everyday life and the global economy.

Benefits of Starting a Tech YouTube Channel

Starting a tech-based YouTube channel offers a wide range of benefits, both financial and personal. Unlike other content niches, tech channels have a unique combination of high engagement, diverse monetization options, and a rapidly expanding audience base.

High CPM and Revenue Potential

Tech content tends to attract advertisers willing to pay a premium to reach a tech-savvy audience. Viewers of tech channels are often in a higher income bracket and are more likely to spend money on technology, making them valuable targets for advertisers. This leads to a higher CPM (Cost Per Thousand Views), which directly increases a creator's ad revenue.

Multiple Monetization Streams

Beyond YouTube ad revenue, tech channels can monetize through several channels-

Affiliate Marketing- Promoting products with affiliate links allows creators to earn a commission from each sale.

Sponsorships- Tech brands are eager to partner with YouTubers to promote their products through reviews and demonstrations.

Merchandising- Successful channels can create branded merchandise or premium content for their audience.

Crowdfunding- Platforms like Patreon allow viewers to support their favorite creators directly.

Global Reach and Influence

Tech content transcends language and geographic barriers. A well-produced video on the latest smartphone or a DIY electronics project can attract viewers from all over the world. YouTube's algorithm promotes engaging and well-optimized content to a global audience, creating the potential for viral growth.

Building a Personal Brand

A successful YouTube channel establishes the creator as an authority in the tech industry. This opens up opportunities beyond YouTube, such as speaking engagements, consulting, and product collaborations.

Passive Income Potential

Once a video is uploaded, it can continue to generate revenue for years through ad views, affiliate sales, and sponsorships. High-quality evergreen content (e.g., "How to Build a Gaming PC" or "Best Budget Smartphones") can provide long-term passive income.

Mindset, Skills, and Tools Needed to Succeed

Running a successful tech channel requires patience, consistency, and a willingness to adapt to changing trends. Unlike viral entertainment content, tech content often takes time to build momentum. Creators need to stay motivated even when early results are slow. Understanding that success is a long-term process rather than an immediate outcome is critical.

Creators should also cultivate a problem-solving mindset. Tech content often revolves around troubleshooting, reviewing, and explaining complex concepts. Being able to think critically and explain solutions clearly is a major advantage.

Essential Skills

Successful tech YouTubers tend to have a combination of technical and creative skills-

Technical Knowledge- A deep understanding of the tech niche, whether it's electronics, coding, AI, or product reviews.

Communication Skills- The ability to explain complex concepts in a simple, engaging manner.

Video Production- Knowledge of camera settings, audio recording, and editing.

Marketing and SEO- Understanding YouTube's algorithm, metadata, and audience behavior.

Community Engagement- Responding to comments and fostering a loyal viewer base.

Tools and Equipment

While some successful channels start with minimal equipment, investing in professional tools can improve video quality and audience engagement. The table below lists essential tools for a tech YouTube channel-

Category	Recommended Tools	Budget Option	Professional Option
Camera	DSLR or smartphone	iPhone 12	Sony Alpha A7 III
Microphone	Lavalier or	Rode	Rode NTG3

Category	Recommended Tools	Budget Option	Professional Option
	shotgun mic	SmartLav+	
Lighting	Softbox or ring light	Neewer 18" Ring Light	Aputure 120D
Editing Software	Video editing suite	iMovie (free)	Adobe Premiere Pro
Screen Capture	Software for tutorials	OBS Studio (free)	Camtasia

Tech-focused YouTube channels have become one of the most lucrative and rapidly growing niches on the platform. The increasing complexity of technology, combined with the growing influence of video-based content, has created a high demand for knowledgeable creators who can simplify and explain tech concepts to a broad audience. By understanding the market dynamics, preparing the right mindset, and investing in essential skills and tools, aspiring creators can establish themselves as authorities in the tech niche and unlock significant financial and professional opportunities. The next chapter will explore how to define a niche and target audience, setting the foundation for long-term success in the competitive world of tech content.

Chapter 2

Defining Your Niche and Target Audience

Building a successful tech-based YouTube channel requires more than just technical knowledge and video production skills. One of the most critical factors that determine long-term success is the ability to define a specific niche and target the right audience. The tech industry is vast and highly competitive, encompassing a wide range of topics including hardware reviews, software tutorials, product unboxing, DIY projects, coding walkthroughs, and emerging technologies. Attempting to cover too broad a range of topics often leads to diluted content and lack of audience connection. In contrast, focusing on a specific niche allows content creators to position themselves as experts in a particular field, build authority, and attract a loyal, engaged audience.

This chapter explores the importance of choosing a specific niche within the tech industry, how to research competitors, identify market gaps, and define the ideal audience for the channel. It also explains how building a community around a focused niche leads to increased viewer retention, stronger engagement, and higher monetization potential. Defining a niche and audience strategy early in the content creation journey provides a clear roadmap for content development and long-term growth.

Why Choosing a Specific Niche Matters

The tech industry is one of the most saturated niches on YouTube. Thousands of creators produce content on similar topics daily, which makes it difficult for new channels to gain visibility and retain viewers. This high level of competition means that simply creating high-quality content is not enough to stand out. The key to success lies in differentiation — offering something unique or specialized that meets an underserved need within the broader tech market.

When a channel focuses on a narrow, well-defined niche, it benefits from several key advantages-

Establishing Authority and Expertise

Viewers are more likely to trust and follow creators who demonstrate deep expertise in a specific area. For instance, a channel dedicated solely to PC building and troubleshooting is more likely to attract an audience interested in computer hardware than a general tech channel covering a wide variety of topics. This concentrated expertise builds credibility and encourages viewers to subscribe and engage consistently.

Algorithmic Advantage

YouTube's recommendation algorithm tends to favor channels that focus on a specific topic. When the algorithm detects that a channel produces consistent content around a certain keyword or topic, it is more likely to recommend that content to viewers interested in that area. This leads to higher search rankings, better visibility, and increased watch time.

Targeted Audience Engagement

A well-defined niche makes it easier to attract an audience with specific interests and needs. When viewers consistently find value in a channel's content, they are more likely to engage through comments, likes, and shares. This type of interaction signals to YouTube's algorithm that the content is valuable, further boosting its visibility.

Higher CPM and Sponsorship Value

Advertisers prefer targeting specific audience segments. A tech channel focused on premium smartphones or high-end gaming PCs is more attractive to advertisers in those markets than a general tech channel. This targeted approach leads to higher CPM (Cost Per Thousand Views) rates and better sponsorship deals.

The table below highlights the difference in CPM rates for various tech niches, reflecting the higher monetization potential of targeted content-

Tech Niche	Average CPM ($)	Audience Engagement Level	Monetization Potential
Smartphone Reviews	8.50 - 12.00	High	High (Premium audience)
DIY Electronics	5.00 - 8.00	Moderate	Moderate
Coding Tutorials	6.00 - 10.00	High	High (Professional audience)
Product Unboxing	4.00 - 6.00	High	Moderate
AI and Automation	9.00 - 15.00	Moderate	High (Emerging market)

As shown in the table, focusing on high-value niches such as AI and automation or smartphone reviews can lead to higher revenue potential, but audience engagement is equally important for sustainable growth.

Identifying the Right Niche

Selecting the right niche requires a balance between personal interest, market demand, and competitive positioning. Creators should focus on areas where they have existing expertise, a genuine passion, and a clear understanding of the target audience's needs.

Personal Interest and Expertise

Creating consistent content over the long term requires motivation and deep understanding of the subject matter. Creators who focus on topics they are passionate about are more likely to sustain creative momentum and provide valuable insights. For instance, a developer with coding experience might naturally gravitate toward coding tutorials, while a hardware enthusiast might prefer PC builds and product reviews.

Market Demand and Trend Analysis

Identifying growing trends within the tech industry helps creators choose niches with high future potential. Platforms like Google Trends, YouTube search data, and social media activity can reveal rising interest in specific topics. For example, AI and automation have shown consistent growth over the last five years, making them attractive niches for new creators.

Competitor Analysis

Researching successful competitors helps identify gaps in the market and differentiate the content strategy. Creators should study competitor content to understand-

- The types of videos that perform well.
- Common audience questions and unmet needs.
- Production quality and presentation style.

Analyzing the top-performing tech channels within a niche provides valuable insights into audience preferences and algorithmic behavior. The table below outlines key competitor analysis factors-

Factor	Example	Purpose
Content Type	"Smartphone Review" videos vs. "Unboxing" videos	Identify which format performs better
Viewer Engagement	High comment activity on troubleshooting videos	Discover what content engages the audience

Factor	Example	Purpose
Channel Growth Rate	10% monthly subscriber growth	Estimate market demand and competition
Video Length	8–12 minutes	Identify optimal video length for retention

Gap Identification

After analyzing competitors and market trends, creators should focus on content gaps. For example, if most smartphone review channels focus on flagship models, a channel dedicated to mid-range or budget smartphones could fill a valuable gap in the market. Similarly, if coding tutorials focus on Python, creating specialized content on emerging languages like Rust or Go could attract a dedicated audience.

Defining the Ideal Audience

Understanding the target audience is as important as defining the content niche. A clear audience profile allows creators to tailor content, tone, and presentation style to viewer preferences.

Audience Profiling

An ideal audience profile should include demographic, psychographic, and behavioral traits. The table below provides an example of an audience profile for a coding tutorial channel-

Trait	Example
Age	18–35 years old
Education Level	High school to college graduates
Interest	Programming, automation, app development
Behavior	Active on YouTube, comments frequently, watches full videos
Preferred Video Length	8–15 minutes

Engagement and Community Building

Audience engagement is critical for channel growth and long-term success. Viewers who feel connected to the creator are more likely to subscribe, share content, and support the channel financially.

Creators should actively engage with their audience through-

Responding to comments and feedback.

Hosting live streams and Q&A sessions.

Encouraging user-generated content and suggestions.

Establishing a sense of community creates a feedback loop where engaged viewers contribute to the channel's success by increasing watch time, boosting engagement signals, and attracting new viewers.

Defining a niche and target audience is a foundational step in building a successful tech YouTube channel. A clear niche allows creators to establish authority, attract targeted viewers, and optimize content for higher engagement and algorithmic performance. Competitor analysis and market research help creators identify gaps and differentiate their content. Audience profiling allows creators to tailor their content and build a loyal community. The combination of niche focus, targeted content strategy, and audience engagement creates a self-reinforcing cycle of growth and profitability. The next chapter will explore how to plan and produce high-quality content that retains viewers and drives long-term success.

Chapter 3

Setting Up Your YouTube Channel

Starting a successful YouTube channel requires more than just uploading videos. A well-optimized and professionally presented channel attracts viewers, builds credibility, and encourages audience retention. First impressions matter, and a visually appealing, well-organized channel sets the foundation for long-term growth. Setting up a YouTube channel involves several critical steps, including creating a YouTube account, designing eye-catching channel art, writing a compelling channel description, and integrating social media and external links. Each of these elements plays a crucial role in attracting viewers, encouraging them to subscribe, and increasing the chances of your content being discovered by YouTube's algorithm.

This chapter provides a detailed, step-by-step guide to setting up a professional YouTube channel. It covers the technical process of account creation, channel customization, and content optimization, ensuring that even first-time creators can follow along. It also includes guidance on creating high-quality graphics, writing engaging copy, and ensuring that all channel elements are aligned with the selected niche and target audience. By the end of this chapter, you will have a fully functional and professional-looking YouTube channel that is ready to attract viewers and start generating engagement.

Creating a YouTube Account

The first step in launching a YouTube channel is creating a YouTube account. Since YouTube is owned by Google, you need to have a Google account to set up a channel. If you already have a Google account, you can use it to create a YouTube channel; otherwise, you will need to set up a new account.

Step 1- Sign in to YouTube

Open a web browser and navigate to www.youtube.com. In the top-right corner of the screen, click the "Sign In" button. You will be redirected to a Google sign-in page. Enter your Google account credentials (email and password) to proceed. If you do not have a Google account, click the "Create account" option and follow the prompts to set up a new Google account.

Step 2- Create a New YouTube Channel

Once signed in, click on your profile icon in the top-right corner of the YouTube homepage. From the drop-down menu, select "Create a Channel." A pop-up window will appear, asking you to choose a name for your channel and upload a profile picture.

You have two options when setting up a YouTube channel-

1. **Personal Channel** – Linked to your personal Google account, using your name or any chosen alias.
2. **Brand Channel** – Managed under a brand account, which allows multiple users to manage the channel under a single entity.

For tech channels, setting up a brand channel is generally the better choice because it provides more customization options, better analytics, and the ability to share channel management with team members.

Naming Your Channel

Choosing the right channel name is essential for brand recognition and discoverability. The name should be memorable, easy to spell, and aligned with the niche and content strategy. Ideally, the name should reflect the type of content you create and appeal to your target audience.

For example, a tech review channel could benefit from a name like **"Tech Unboxed"** or **"Gadget Insight."** A coding tutorial channel might work well with a name like **"CodeSphere"** or **"DevStation."**

The table below outlines naming strategies based on different tech niches-

Niche	Example Names	Reasoning

Niche	Example Names	Reasoning
Smartphone Reviews	Tech Unboxed, Mobile Insider	Reflects the type of content and tech focus
Coding Tutorials	CodeSphere, DevStation	Simple, professional, and easy to remember
PC Builds	BuildBytes, TechRig	Highlights the building aspect and tech focus
AI & Automation	AI Insider, FutureCode	Reflects cutting-edge tech and automation focus

Ensure that the channel name is available across social media platforms to maintain consistent branding. Tools like Namechk or BrandSnag can help verify availability.

Setting Up Channel Art

Professional channel art increases the credibility and visual appeal of your channel. Channel art includes the profile picture, banner, and video thumbnails. Consistency in design creates a cohesive brand identity, making your channel more recognizable and professional.

Profile Picture

The profile picture should be simple yet distinctive. Many tech channels use a logo or an icon related to the niche. For personal branding, using a high-quality headshot works well. The recommended size for a YouTube profile picture is **800 x 800 pixels**.

Banner

The banner (or channel header) is displayed at the top of your YouTube page. It provides a large space for branding, channel information, and promotional messages. A clean, high-resolution image that reflects your niche and content style is ideal.

Recommended banner size- 2560 x 1440 pixels. **Safe display area-** Keep critical text and logos within 1546 x 423 pixels to ensure they are visible on all devices.

A sample banner design for a tech channel focused on coding tutorials might include-

- A background featuring code snippets or a keyboard.
- The channel name displayed in a modern, bold font.
- A tagline such as "Master Coding with Expert Tutorials."

Thumbnails

Custom thumbnails increase click-through rates. Each thumbnail should have a consistent style, including the same color palette, font, and design elements. The recommended size for a thumbnail is **1280 x 720 pixels**.

Writing an Engaging Channel Description

The channel description introduces new viewers to your content and helps YouTube's algorithm understand the channel's focus. The description should be informative, engaging, and optimized for search.

An effective description includes-

- A clear statement of the channel's purpose and niche.
- Keywords related to the content to improve discoverability.
- A call to action encouraging viewers to subscribe.

Example-
"Welcome to CodeSphere — your go-to channel for coding tutorials, automation hacks, and programming insights. Whether you're a beginner or an experienced developer, you'll find step-by-step guides and real-world projects to elevate your coding skills. Subscribe now to stay updated with weekly content!"

The description should also include links to relevant social media platforms and a professional email for business inquiries.

Adding Links to Social Media and Websites

Integrating social media links increases cross-platform engagement and provides additional touchpoints for your audience. In the channel customization section, there is an option to add up to five links to the channel banner. These links can include-

- A personal or business website.
- Instagram, Twitter, or LinkedIn profiles.
- Patreon or Ko-Fi for crowdfunding.
- A merchandise store.

To add links-

1. Go to **YouTube Studio**.
2. Navigate to the **Customization** tab.
3. Select **Basic Info**.
4. Enter the desired link titles and URLs.
5. Click **Publish** to update the changes.

Adding a website link helps direct viewers to additional content, services, or products, creating more opportunities for monetization.

Channel Customization and Settings

In YouTube Studio, the customization section allows for additional settings that improve the channel's functionality and presentation-

Channel Trailer- Upload a short video introducing your channel's purpose and content style.

Featured Videos- Highlight popular or recent uploads to increase visibility.

Playlist Organization- Group similar videos into playlists for easier navigation.

Tags and Keywords- Include relevant keywords to improve searchability and algorithmic ranking.

Setting up a YouTube channel involves more than just creating an account and uploading content. A professional and well-organized channel increases viewer trust, encourages subscriptions, and improves algorithmic visibility. A strong channel name, consistent channel art, an engaging description, and properly integrated links create a cohesive and attractive online presence. Following these steps ensures that your channel is not only visually appealing but also strategically positioned for long-term growth. In the next chapter, we will explore how to plan and produce high-quality content that resonates with your audience and maximizes engagement.

Chapter 4

Essential Equipment and Tools

Creating high-quality content for a tech-focused YouTube channel requires not only knowledge and creativity but also the right equipment. High production quality enhances viewer engagement and retention, making the difference between a channel that attracts loyal subscribers and one that struggles to gain traction. Viewers expect crisp video resolution, clear audio, professional lighting, and smooth camera work. Poor production quality, such as low-resolution video or distorted sound, can drive viewers away, even if the content itself is valuable.

Investing in the right tools helps achieve a professional look and feel without necessarily requiring a large budget. While many successful YouTubers start with basic equipment, upgrading over time as the channel grows ensures a steady increase in production quality. This chapter provides a comprehensive guide to the essential equipment needed for producing high-quality tech videos, including cameras, microphones, lighting setups, tripods, screen recording software, and video editing tools. It also compares budget-friendly options with professional-grade alternatives, helping you make informed decisions based on your current budget and production goals.

Cameras

The camera is the most critical piece of equipment for any YouTube channel. The quality of the video directly impacts viewer perception, and high-resolution, sharp, and well-lit footage makes your content more appealing. There are several types of cameras to choose from, including DSLR cameras, smartphones, and webcams. Each has distinct advantages and trade-offs depending on your budget and filming requirements.

DSLR and Mirrorless Cameras

DSLR and mirrorless cameras provide professional-quality video with excellent control over focus, exposure, and depth of field. They are ideal for tech videos involving product reviews, unboxings, or DIY builds, where close-up shots and detailed focus are essential. DSLR cameras typically offer superior low-light performance and interchangeable lenses, which allows for greater creative flexibility.

Feature	DSLR Cameras	Mirrorless Cameras
Lens Compatibility	Supports a wide range of lenses	Also supports multiple lenses but typically smaller

Feature	DSLR Cameras	Mirrorless Cameras
Autofocus Speed	Slower but precise	Fast and highly accurate
Size and Weight	Larger and heavier	Compact and lightweight
Battery Life	Longer	Shorter
Price Range	$500–$3000+	$600–$4000+

For a tech-focused channel, a mirrorless camera like the **Sony A6400** or **Canon EOS M50** provides a perfect balance between image quality and ease of use. These cameras offer 4K resolution and excellent autofocus capabilities, which are ideal for capturing detailed product shots and recording high-quality tutorials.

Smartphones

Modern smartphones are equipped with high-resolution cameras that can rival entry-level DSLR and mirrorless cameras in terms of quality. Many flagship models, such as the **iPhone 15 Pro** and **Samsung Galaxy S24 Ultra**, support 4K recording, optical image stabilization, and wide dynamic range. Smartphones are highly convenient for on-the-go filming or quick setup scenarios.

The table below highlights the differences between high-end smartphones and dedicated cameras-

Feature	Smartphone Cameras	Dedicated Cameras
Portability	Extremely portable	Less portable
Lens Options	Fixed lens	Interchangeable lenses available
Image Quality in Low Light	Decent with computational photography	Superior with larger sensors
Price	$800–$1500	$500–$4000

Smartphones are a great starting point for tech content creators on a budget. Pairing a smartphone with a tripod and an external microphone significantly improves the overall production value.

Webcams

Webcams are affordable and easy to set up, making them suitable for streaming and screen-based tutorials. High-end models, such as the **Logitech Brio**

4K, offer excellent resolution and frame rates, but they lack the depth of field and creative flexibility of DSLR or mirrorless cameras. Webcams are ideal for recording coding tutorials, product overviews, and live Q&A sessions.

Microphones

Good audio quality is often more important than video quality. Poor sound can drive viewers away even if the video is visually appealing. There are two main types of microphones to consider- condenser microphones and dynamic microphones.

Condenser Microphones

Condenser microphones are highly sensitive and capture detailed sound with a wide frequency range. They are ideal for quiet environments where audio clarity is a priority. USB condenser microphones like the **Blue Yeti** or **Rode NT-USB** are popular among YouTubers because of their plug-and-play simplicity and high-quality output.

Dynamic Microphones

Dynamic microphones are less sensitive to background noise, making them ideal for noisy environments. They are commonly used for live streaming and voiceovers. The **Shure SM7B** is a professional-grade dynamic microphone widely used by podcasters and YouTubers for its warm, natural sound.

Feature	Condenser Microphones	Dynamic Microphones
Sensitivity	High	Low
Background Noise Rejection	Low	High
Power Requirement	Requires phantom power (XLR models)	No additional power required
Best Use Case	Voiceovers, tutorials, quiet environments	Streaming, noisy environments

Lighting

Proper lighting enhances video clarity and reduces shadows, making your content look professional. There are three main types of lighting used for YouTube videos- softbox lights, ring lights, and natural lighting.

Softbox Lights

Softbox lights produce diffused, natural-looking light that reduces harsh shadows. They are ideal for product reviews and tutorial videos.

Ring Lights

Ring lights provide even lighting and create a flattering catchlight effect in the eyes. They are ideal for talking-head videos.

Natural Lighting

Natural light is free and accessible but inconsistent. Shooting near a large window during daylight hours provides soft, even light, but weather changes can disrupt consistency.

Tripods and Stabilizers

A stable camera improves video quality by eliminating shakiness. Tripods are essential for stationary shots, while gimbals and stabilizers allow for smooth movement during handheld filming. Budget options like the **AmazonBasics Tripod** work well for static shots, while the **DJI Ronin-S** is a professional-grade gimbal ideal for dynamic shots.

Screen Recording Software

For tech tutorials and coding videos, screen recording software is essential. OBS Studio (Open Broadcaster Software) is a free, open-source platform that allows multi-source recording, overlays, and live streaming. Camtasia offers a user-friendly interface with built-in editing tools.

Video Editing Software

Post-production editing enhances video quality and creates a polished final product. Popular options include-

Adobe Premiere Pro – Industry-standard, highly versatile.

Final Cut Pro – Mac-exclusive, optimized for Apple hardware.

DaVinci Resolve – Professional-grade color correction and editing (free and paid versions).

Software	Platform	Best Use Case	Price
Adobe Premiere Pro	Windows, Mac	Professional editing, multi-camera	$20.99/month

Software	Platform	Best Use Case	Price
Final Cut Pro	Mac	Fast rendering, Apple integration	$299 one-time
DaVinci Resolve	Windows, Mac, Linux	Color grading, professional use	Free/$295

Budget Options vs. Professional Equipment

Balancing budget and quality is critical for new YouTubers. The table below outlines a sample budget-friendly and professional-grade setup for a tech YouTube channel-

Equipment	Budget Option	Professional Option
Camera	iPhone 15 Pro	Sony A6400
Microphone	Blue Yeti	Shure SM7B
Lighting	Ring Light	Softbox Kit
Tripod	AmazonBasics Tripod	DJI Ronin-S
Editing Software	DaVinci Resolve (Free)	Adobe Premiere Pro

Investing in high-quality equipment elevates your content, improves viewer engagement, and increases channel growth potential. Cameras, microphones, lighting, and editing software collectively shape the overall production value. Balancing affordability and quality is key, with smartphones and budget microphones serving as entry points while professional-grade tools unlock greater creative potential. In the next chapter, we will explore how to plan and produce engaging tech content that captivates viewers and builds a loyal subscriber base.

Chapter 4

Essential Equipment and Tools

Creating high-quality content for a tech-focused YouTube channel requires not only knowledge and creativity but also the right equipment. High production quality enhances viewer engagement and retention, making the difference between a channel that attracts loyal subscribers and one that struggles to gain traction. Viewers expect crisp video resolution, clear audio, professional lighting, and smooth camera work. Poor production quality, such as low-resolution video or distorted sound, can drive viewers away, even if the content itself is valuable.

Investing in the right tools helps achieve a professional look and feel without necessarily requiring a large budget. While many successful YouTubers start with basic equipment, upgrading over time as the channel grows ensures a steady increase in production quality. This chapter provides a comprehensive guide to the essential equipment needed for producing high-quality tech videos, including cameras, microphones, lighting setups, tripods, screen recording software, and video editing tools. It also compares budget-friendly options with professional-grade alternatives, helping you make informed decisions based on your current budget and production goals.

Cameras

The camera is the most critical piece of equipment for any YouTube channel. The quality of the video directly impacts viewer perception, and high-resolution, sharp, and well-lit footage makes your content more appealing. There are several types of cameras to choose from, including DSLR cameras, smartphones, and webcams. Each has distinct advantages and trade-offs depending on your budget and filming requirements.

DSLR and Mirrorless Cameras

DSLR and mirrorless cameras provide professional-quality video with excellent control over focus, exposure, and depth of field. They are ideal for tech videos involving product reviews, unboxings, or DIY builds, where close-up shots and detailed focus are essential. DSLR cameras typically offer superior low-light performance and interchangeable lenses, which allows for greater creative flexibility.

Feature	DSLR Cameras	Mirrorless Cameras
Lens Compatibility	Supports a wide range of lenses	Also supports multiple lenses but typically smaller

Feature	DSLR Cameras	Mirrorless Cameras
Autofocus Speed	Slower but precise	Fast and highly accurate
Size and Weight	Larger and heavier	Compact and lightweight
Battery Life	Longer	Shorter
Price Range	$500–$3000+	$600–$4000+

For a tech-focused channel, a mirrorless camera like the **Sony A6400** or **Canon EOS M50** provides a perfect balance between image quality and ease of use. These cameras offer 4K resolution and excellent autofocus capabilities, which are ideal for capturing detailed product shots and recording high-quality tutorials.

Smartphones

Modern smartphones are equipped with high-resolution cameras that can rival entry-level DSLR and mirrorless cameras in terms of quality. Many flagship models, such as the **iPhone 15 Pro** and **Samsung Galaxy S24 Ultra**, support 4K recording, optical image stabilization, and wide dynamic range. Smartphones are highly convenient for on-the-go filming or quick setup scenarios.

The table below highlights the differences between high-end smartphones and dedicated cameras-

Feature	Smartphone Cameras	Dedicated Cameras
Portability	Extremely portable	Less portable
Lens Options	Fixed lens	Interchangeable lenses available
Image Quality in Low Light	Decent with computational photography	Superior with larger sensors
Price	$800–$1500	$500–$4000

Smartphones are a great starting point for tech content creators on a budget. Pairing a smartphone with a tripod and an external microphone significantly improves the overall production value.

Webcams

Webcams are affordable and easy to set up, making them suitable for streaming and screen-based tutorials. High-end models, such as the **Logitech Brio**

4K, offer excellent resolution and frame rates, but they lack the depth of field and creative flexibility of DSLR or mirrorless cameras. Webcams are ideal for recording coding tutorials, product overviews, and live Q&A sessions.

Microphones

Good audio quality is often more important than video quality. Poor sound can drive viewers away even if the video is visually appealing. There are two main types of microphones to consider- condenser microphones and dynamic microphones.

Condenser Microphones

Condenser microphones are highly sensitive and capture detailed sound with a wide frequency range. They are ideal for quiet environments where audio clarity is a priority. USB condenser microphones like the **Blue Yeti** or **Rode NT-USB** are popular among YouTubers because of their plug-and-play simplicity and high-quality output.

Dynamic Microphones

Dynamic microphones are less sensitive to background noise, making them ideal for noisy environments. They are commonly used for live streaming and voiceovers. The **Shure SM7B** is a professional-grade dynamic microphone widely used by podcasters and YouTubers for its warm, natural sound.

Feature	Condenser Microphones	Dynamic Microphones
Sensitivity	High	Low
Background Noise Rejection	Low	High
Power Requirement	Requires phantom power (XLR models)	No additional power required
Best Use Case	Voiceovers, tutorials, quiet environments	Streaming, noisy environments

Lighting

Proper lighting enhances video clarity and reduces shadows, making your content look professional. There are three main types of lighting used for YouTube videos- softbox lights, ring lights, and natural lighting.

Softbox Lights

Softbox lights produce diffused, natural-looking light that reduces harsh shadows. They are ideal for product reviews and tutorial videos.

Ring Lights

Ring lights provide even lighting and create a flattering catchlight effect in the eyes. They are ideal for talking-head videos.

Natural Lighting

Natural light is free and accessible but inconsistent. Shooting near a large window during daylight hours provides soft, even light, but weather changes can disrupt consistency.

Tripods and Stabilizers

A stable camera improves video quality by eliminating shakiness. Tripods are essential for stationary shots, while gimbals and stabilizers allow for smooth movement during handheld filming. Budget options like the **AmazonBasics Tripod** work well for static shots, while the **DJI Ronin-S** is a professional-grade gimbal ideal for dynamic shots.

Screen Recording Software

For tech tutorials and coding videos, screen recording software is essential. OBS Studio (Open Broadcaster Software) is a free, open-source platform that allows multi-source recording, overlays, and live streaming. Camtasia offers a user-friendly interface with built-in editing tools.

Video Editing Software

Post-production editing enhances video quality and creates a polished final product. Popular options include-

- **Adobe Premiere Pro** – Industry-standard, highly versatile.
- **Final Cut Pro** – Mac-exclusive, optimized for Apple hardware.
- **DaVinci Resolve** – Professional-grade color correction and editing (free and paid versions).

Software	Platform	Best Use Case	Price
Adobe Premiere Pro	Windows, Mac	Professional editing, multi-camera	$20.99/month

Software	Platform	Best Use Case	Price
Final Cut Pro	Mac	Fast rendering, Apple integration	$299 one-time
DaVinci Resolve	Windows, Mac, Linux	Color grading, professional use	Free/$295

Budget Options vs. Professional Equipment

Balancing budget and quality is critical for new YouTubers. The table below outlines a sample budget-friendly and professional-grade setup for a tech YouTube channel-

Equipment	Budget Option	Professional Option
Camera	iPhone 15 Pro	Sony A6400
Microphone	Blue Yeti	Shure SM7B
Lighting	Ring Light	Softbox Kit
Tripod	AmazonBasics Tripod	DJI Ronin-S
Editing Software	DaVinci Resolve (Free)	Adobe Premiere Pro

Investing in high-quality equipment elevates your content, improves viewer engagement, and increases channel growth potential. Cameras, microphones, lighting, and editing software collectively shape the overall production value. Balancing affordability and quality is key, with smartphones and budget microphones serving as entry points while professional-grade tools unlock greater creative potential. In the next chapter, we will explore how to plan and produce engaging tech content that captivates viewers and builds a loyal subscriber base.

Chapter 5

Planning and Scripting Tech Videos

Creating engaging and high-quality tech content for YouTube requires more than just technical knowledge and good equipment. Effective planning and scripting form the backbone of successful video production. A well-structured and thoughtfully planned video ensures that your message is clear, engaging, and easy for viewers to follow. Randomly filming without a script or plan often leads to confusing, disorganized content that fails to capture or retain audience attention. Planning and scripting not only help in improving the overall flow and delivery of the video but also ensure that key points are communicated effectively, reducing the chances of mistakes or wasted recording time.

Many successful YouTubers follow a structured approach when creating their content. They begin by conducting thorough research, followed by writing a clear and engaging script. The script helps maintain a consistent flow and ensures that the content remains focused and valuable to the target audience. A strong script also makes the editing process more manageable and increases the likelihood of viewer engagement through clear and actionable communication. This chapter explores the process of researching and planning video content, structuring it effectively, and creating a compelling script. It also includes sample scripts for various types of tech videos to give you a practical understanding of how to apply these techniques.

Researching and Planning Video Content

The first step in creating a successful tech video is thorough research and planning. Without proper research, the content may lack depth, accuracy, or relevance, leading to reduced credibility and viewer engagement. Research involves understanding the target audience's interests, identifying gaps in existing content, and ensuring that the information provided is accurate and up to date.

Understanding Your Target Audience

Understanding the target audience is essential for tailoring the content to their interests and technical knowledge level. A video aimed at professional developers will have a different tone and complexity than a video aimed at tech enthusiasts or beginners. For example, a video about setting up a Raspberry Pi should assume different baseline knowledge depending on whether the target audience is students, hobbyists, or professionals.

Audience Type	Content Focus	Technical Depth	Preferred Style
Beginners	Basic tutorials, unboxing, product overviews	Low to Medium	Informal, simple explanations

Audience Type	Content Focus	Technical Depth	Preferred Style
Intermediate	How-to guides, troubleshooting, comparisons	Medium to High	Balanced, instructional
Advanced	In-depth technical reviews, industry trends, deep dives	High	Professional, precise language

Researching Competitors

Analyzing competitor content helps identify what works and what doesn't within the niche. Watching similar videos reveals common patterns, popular topics, and audience engagement tactics. Look for unanswered questions in the comments section or gaps in the information provided by competitors. For example, if most videos on "Raspberry Pi setup" focus on the hardware aspect but neglect the software configuration, creating a detailed video on software installation and troubleshooting could attract a dedicated audience.

Selecting a Unique Angle

A unique perspective sets your video apart from competitors. Presenting a different angle or including additional value helps in building a loyal subscriber base. For example, instead of making a generic "Best Programming Laptops" video, a more engaging angle could be "Best Laptops for Python Developers Under $1000." This makes the content more specific and appealing to a niche audience.

Structuring Video Content

A well-structured video maintains audience attention and ensures clear communication of key points. A logical flow enhances viewer understanding and engagement. Most successful YouTube videos follow a three-part structure-

Introduction

The introduction sets the tone for the video and immediately communicates what the audience can expect. It should grab the viewer's attention within the first 10–15 seconds, as viewer retention typically drops off sharply after this period if the content fails to engage. The introduction should include a brief summary of the topic, why it matters, and what the viewer will gain from watching the video.

For example, an introduction for a video titled **"How to Overclock a Raspberry Pi"** could be-

"Are you looking to get more power from your Raspberry Pi without damaging the hardware? In this video, I'm going to show you how to safely overclock your Raspberry Pi to increase performance by up to 20% — without overheating or stability issues. Let's get started!"

Body

The body contains the core content and should be structured logically. Breaking down the content into clear, manageable segments improves understanding. If the video involves a tutorial, a step-by-step format with on-screen guidance works well. For tech reviews, covering features, pros and cons, and practical demonstrations keeps the content engaging.

Use transitions between segments to maintain flow. For example, instead of abruptly switching from explaining CPU overclocking to cooling solutions, a smooth transition would be-

"Now that we've increased the clock speed, let's talk about keeping the Raspberry Pi cool to prevent performance throttling."

The conclusion summarizes the key takeaways and provides a clear call to action. Encouraging viewers to like, subscribe, and comment helps increase engagement and channel growth. For example-

"Now you know how to safely overclock your Raspberry Pi for improved performance. If you found this video helpful, make sure to hit the like button and subscribe for more tech tips and tutorials. Drop a comment below if you have any questions or if you'd like to see more overclocking videos!"

Writing Engaging Scripts

An effective script provides a clear roadmap for the video and ensures that no important details are overlooked. A conversational tone works best for YouTube, as it makes the content more relatable and easier to understand. The script should balance technical accuracy with accessibility to prevent alienating less experienced viewers.

Sample Script for a Tech Tutorial

Title- *How to Set Up a Raspberry Pi for Beginners*

Introduction-
"Hi everyone! Welcome back to the channel. Today, I'm going to show you how to set up a Raspberry Pi from scratch. Whether you're a complete beginner or looking to troubleshoot a tricky setup, this guide will cover everything you need to know. Let's dive in!"

Body-

"First, let's start by gathering the required materials. You'll need a Raspberry Pi board, a microSD card, a power supply, and an HDMI cable. Insert the microSD card into your computer and open the Raspberry Pi Imager tool. Select the latest version of Raspberry Pi OS and click 'Write.' Once that's done, remove the microSD card and insert it into your Raspberry Pi.

"Next, connect the HDMI cable to your monitor and plug in the power supply. The Raspberry Pi should boot up automatically. If the screen remains blank, check the cable connection and try restarting the board.

"Now let's configure the OS. Open the terminal and type 'sudo raspi-config.' Navigate to the localization settings and select your country and keyboard layout. Finally, enable SSH if you plan to access the Raspberry Pi remotely."

Conclusion-

"That's it — you've successfully set up your Raspberry Pi! If you found this video helpful, please give it a thumbs up and consider subscribing for more Raspberry Pi tutorials and project ideas. See you in the next video!"

Sample Script for a Tech Review

Title- *Best Laptops for Programming in 2025*

Introduction-

"Are you a developer looking for the perfect laptop? In this video, I'll review the top five programming laptops for 2025 based on performance, battery life, and price. Let's get started!"

Body-

"First on the list is the MacBook Pro M2. It features a powerful M2 chip, 16GB of RAM, and a 512GB SSD, making it perfect for compiling large codebases. The battery life is also impressive, lasting up to 20 hours on a single charge."

Conclusion-

"That's my list of the best programming laptops for 2025. If you've used any of these, let me know your thoughts in the comments. Don't forget to like and subscribe for more tech reviews!"

Planning and scripting are crucial for producing high-quality tech videos. Effective research ensures that the content is relevant and valuable to the target audience. Structuring the video with a strong introduction, informative body, and clear conclusion helps maintain viewer engagement and deliver a consistent message. Writing a compelling script keeps the video focused, improves delivery, and reduces editing time. In the next chapter, we will explore how to film and edit your videos to achieve a professional look and feel.

Chapter 6

Filming High-Quality Tech Videos

Creating a successful tech YouTube channel requires more than just having valuable content and a clear script — the way the video is filmed plays a crucial role in determining its success. High-quality visuals, clear audio, and effective lighting are essential elements that keep viewers engaged and build a professional image for the channel. Poor production quality, such as low-resolution video, shaky footage, or bad audio, can undermine even the most informative content, leading to reduced watch time and lower subscriber growth.

Filming a tech video involves a combination of technical and creative skills. Understanding camera settings, audio setup, lighting adjustments, and proper camera angles allows you to produce professional-quality videos that stand out in the crowded tech niche. The goal is to create a seamless viewing experience where the audience can focus on the content rather than being distracted by poor production quality.

This chapter provides a step-by-step guide on recording high-quality tech videos, covering camera setup, audio recording, lighting techniques, and filming strategies for different types of tech videos, including hardware reviews, product unboxings, and software tutorials.

Setting Up the Camera

Choosing the right camera and understanding its settings is the foundation of producing high-quality tech videos. While professional YouTubers often use high-end DSLR or mirrorless cameras, beginners can still produce excellent content using a smartphone or a webcam, provided the settings are optimized correctly.

Camera Types and Recommendations

The type of camera used will affect the overall look and feel of the video. DSLR and mirrorless cameras provide the highest image quality and offer greater flexibility with lens choices and depth of field. Smartphones have improved dramatically in video quality over recent years and are often equipped with features such as 4K recording and optical image stabilization. Webcams are convenient for recording screen-based content like software tutorials, but they typically lack the sharpness and color depth of dedicated cameras.

Camera Type	Pros	Cons	Best Use Case
DSLR	High resolution, interchangeable lenses, professional	Expensive, bulky, requires technical	Hardware reviews, product

Camera Type	Pros	Cons	Best Use Case
	depth of field	knowledge	demonstrations
Mirrorless	Lighter than DSLRs, fast autofocus, high image quality	High cost, shorter battery life	General-purpose tech videos, reviews
Smartphone	Portable, 4K recording, easy to use	Limited lens options, overheating issues	Vlogs, quick tutorials
Webcam	Convenient, plug-and-play, good for streaming	Lower resolution, limited color depth	Software tutorials, live streaming

Optimal Camera Settings

Once the camera is selected, adjusting the settings correctly ensures that the video quality meets professional standards.

Resolution- Recording in 1080p (Full HD) is the industry standard for YouTube videos, but recording in 4K provides sharper details and better flexibility in post-production. Even if the final video is exported in 1080p, shooting in 4K allows for better cropping and stabilization.

Frame Rate- A frame rate of 30 fps (frames per second) works well for most content. For slow-motion or high-action videos, recording at 60 fps or higher is preferable.

Shutter Speed- The shutter speed should be set to double the frame rate for natural motion blur. For example, if recording at 30 fps, the shutter speed should be set to 1/60.

ISO- Keep the ISO as low as possible to reduce noise in the video. A value between 100 and 400 works well in most lighting conditions.

White Balance- Adjust the white balance manually to match the lighting conditions and prevent color shifts. Most cameras have presets for daylight, shade, and indoor lighting.

Focus- Autofocus works well for dynamic shots but can hunt and create distracting shifts. Manual focus provides more consistent results, especially for close-up shots of hardware.

Audio Setup

High-quality audio is often more important than video quality in tech content. Viewers are more likely to tolerate lower video resolution than poor audio. A crisp, clear sound ensures that the content remains easy to follow and professional.

Microphone Types and Recommendations

The type of microphone used significantly impacts audio quality. Built-in camera microphones often produce poor sound quality due to background noise and limited frequency response. External microphones provide cleaner, more accurate audio.

Microphone Type	Pros	Cons	Best Use Case
Lavalier (Clip-On)	Portable, hands-free, good for consistent volume	Can pick up clothing noise, lower sound depth	Product demos, tutorials
Shotgun	Directional, excellent sound isolation	Bulky, requires precise positioning	Reviews, voiceovers
Condenser	High sensitivity, captures detailed sound	Requires external power, sensitive to background noise	Voiceovers, commentary
Dynamic	Excellent background	Lower sensitivity,	Live streaming, noisy

Microphone Type	Pros	Cons	Best Use Case
	noise rejection	limited high-frequency capture	environments

Audio Recording Techniques

Position the microphone close to the mouth (6–12 inches) for clear audio while avoiding plosive sounds. If using a shotgun mic, point it toward the mouth but avoid placing it too close, as it may pick up breathing noises. When recording voiceovers, use a pop filter to reduce harsh "P" and "B" sounds. Record a few seconds of ambient noise at the start of each session to make it easier to clean up background noise during editing.

Lighting Setup

Proper lighting enhances video clarity and creates a professional look. Even the best camera will produce poor-quality video under inadequate lighting conditions.

Types of Lighting

Soft lighting reduces shadows and highlights details better than harsh lighting. Natural light is ideal, but consistent results are easier to achieve using artificial lighting.

Lighting Type	Pros	Cons	Best Use Case
Softbox	Soft, even light, reduces shadows	Requires space, not very portable	Product reviews, unboxings
Ring Light	Direct, even light on the subject	Can create reflections in glasses	Face-focused videos, vlogging
LED Panel	Adjustable brightness and color temperature	More expensive	All-purpose lighting

Three-Point Lighting Setup

The three-point lighting setup is a standard technique used in professional video production-

Key Light- Positioned at a 45-degree angle from the subject to provide the primary light source.

Fill Light- Positioned opposite the key light to reduce shadows.

Backlight- Positioned behind the subject to create separation from the background and add depth.

Camera Angles and Framing

Effective camera angles improve video composition and viewer engagement. For product reviews, a combination of close-ups, wide shots, and overhead angles works well. For software tutorials, a direct shot of the presenter combined with screen recording creates a balanced viewing experience.

Types of Shots and When to Use Them

Wide Shot- Introduces the subject and sets the context.

Medium Shot- Focuses on the presenter and maintains engagement.

Close-Up- Highlights details, such as hardware ports or screen settings.

Overhead Shot- Ideal for product unboxing and demonstrations.

Filming Strategies

Hardware Reviews

Use a combination of close-ups and wide shots to showcase the product's design and features. Use a turntable for smooth rotational shots of the hardware. Include on-screen text or graphics to highlight key specifications.

Product Unboxings

Start with a wide shot to introduce the packaging. Switch to close-ups while opening the box to capture the product's details. Maintain consistent lighting to prevent color shifts.

Software Tutorials

Use screen recording software like OBS or Camtasia to capture the process. Include a picture-in-picture window with the presenter's face to maintain a personal connection. Use mouse highlighting and zoom effects to direct attention to key actions.

Filming high-quality tech videos requires a strategic combination of proper camera setup, clear audio, balanced lighting, and effective framing. Understanding the best equipment and techniques for different types of tech videos ensures that the final product meets professional standards. By mastering these filming techniques, you create a polished, engaging viewing experience that strengthens your channel's credibility and keeps viewers coming back for more. In the next chapter, we will explore how to edit and enhance these videos to make them ready for publishing.

Chapter 7

Editing and Post-Production

Producing a high-quality tech video does not end once the filming is complete. The editing and post-production phase is where raw footage is transformed into a polished, professional video that engages viewers and communicates information clearly. Editing is a creative and technical process that requires attention to detail, patience, and the right software tools. Successful editing enhances the flow of the video, removes distractions, improves audio quality, and adds professional touches such as transitions, background music, and color grading.

Effective editing ensures that the final video maintains a consistent tone and style, reinforcing the channel's identity and branding. A well-edited video not only retains viewer attention but also encourages increased watch time — a critical factor in YouTube's algorithm for recommending videos. Furthermore, smooth editing improves the viewing experience by eliminating awkward pauses, improving audio clarity, and guiding the viewer's attention toward key elements.

This chapter provides a comprehensive guide to the video editing process, covering everything from cutting and trimming footage to adding professional intros, enhancing audio, and optimizing the final file for YouTube. Mastering these editing techniques ensures that your tech videos are polished, engaging, and visually appealing.

Cutting and Trimming Footage

The first step in the editing process involves cutting and trimming the raw footage to remove unnecessary content, fix mistakes, and create a smooth flow. Raw footage is rarely perfect — there may be instances of long pauses, off-topic comments, or technical errors that need to be removed.

Cutting refers to splitting a video clip into separate sections, while trimming involves removing unwanted parts from the beginning, middle, or end of a clip. Most video editing software provides a simple timeline-based interface where you can easily cut and trim clips.

Process for Cutting and Trimming

1. Import the raw video files into the editing software.
2. Place the clips onto the editing timeline.
3. Watch the entire video and mark the sections where cuts or trims are required.
4. Use the cutting tool to split the video at the desired points.
5. Remove the unnecessary sections and adjust the remaining clips to create a seamless flow.
6. Ensure that there are no abrupt cuts by adding subtle transitions or fading effects where necessary.

Cutting and trimming are essential for improving the pacing of the video. Viewers tend to lose interest quickly if a video is too slow or contains too much filler content. A well-paced video maintains viewer engagement and improves watch time — a key metric for YouTube's algorithm.

Adding Effects and Transitions

After cutting and trimming the video, the next step is to add effects and transitions to create a professional look and smooth flow between scenes. Transitions help prevent jarring jumps between clips and make the video feel cohesive.

Effects can be used to highlight specific details, such as zooming in on a product or emphasizing key points in a software tutorial. However, overusing effects can make the video feel unprofessional and distracting. The goal is to use transitions and effects sparingly to enhance — not overwhelm — the content.

Transition Types and When to Use Them

Transition Type	Description	Best Use Case
Cut	Direct switch from one clip to another	Fast-paced content, tutorials
Fade In/Out	Gradually increases or decreases brightness	Starting or ending a video, transitioning between topics
Dissolve	Blends two clips together for a smooth transition	Product reviews, hardware demonstrations
Slide	Slides one clip out while introducing the next	Tutorials, step-by-step instructions
Zoom	Gradually magnifies a specific part of the screen	Highlighting key details in hardware or software

Process for Adding Transitions and Effects

1. Drag and drop the transition effect between two clips on the timeline.
2. Adjust the duration of the transition to avoid making it too fast or too slow.
3. Apply effects selectively — zoom into the product during a hardware review or highlight a specific UI element in a software tutorial.
4. Preview the video to ensure the transitions and effects feel natural and do not disrupt the flow.

Enhancing Audio Quality

Clear audio is critical for a successful tech video. Even if the video quality is excellent, poor audio can ruin the viewing experience and lead to increased drop-off rates. Enhancing audio quality involves adjusting volume levels, removing background noise, and adding sound effects to create a professional listening experience.

Audio Enhancement Techniques

Noise Reduction- Background noise, such as fan noise or traffic sounds, can be reduced using noise reduction tools available in most editing software. Adobe Premiere Pro, Final Cut Pro, and DaVinci Resolve all include built-in noise reduction filters.

Volume Normalization- Ensuring that the audio levels remain consistent throughout the video prevents the need for the viewer to constantly adjust the volume. Use the audio normalization feature to maintain even levels.

Equalization (EQ)- Adjust the treble and bass levels to make the voice sound clear and natural.

Compression- Apply compression to reduce sudden volume spikes and balance the overall audio profile.

Ideal Audio Levels for YouTube

Audio Type	Target Level
Dialogue	-6 dB to -12 dB
Background Music	-20 dB to -30 dB
Sound Effects	-10 dB to -15 dB

Creating Professional Intros and Outros

A strong intro grabs the viewer's attention and sets the tone for the video. A polished outro encourages viewers to like, subscribe, and engage with other content on the channel.

Best Practices for Intros

- Keep the intro short (5 to 10 seconds).
- Include the channel logo and a clear statement of the video's topic.
- Add engaging music that fits the channel's tone and niche.

Best Practices for Outros

- Include a call to action ("Like and Subscribe!").
- Display links to other videos or playlists.
- Use an animated end screen with subscribe buttons and video previews.

Adding Background Music and Sound Effects

Background music adds mood and personality to the video. It should complement the content without overpowering the dialogue. Sound effects, such as clicks or beeps, help draw attention to key actions in software tutorials or highlight product features in hardware reviews.

Best Practices for Background Music and Sound Effects

- Use royalty-free music from platforms like YouTube Audio Library or Epidemic Sound.

- Keep the background music volume lower than the dialogue.
- Avoid music with distracting lyrics.

Color Correction and Grading

Color correction involves adjusting the video's color balance, contrast, and exposure to create a consistent look. Color grading gives the video a specific style or mood.

Color Correction Techniques

- Adjust the white balance to eliminate unnatural color tones.
- Increase contrast to make the video more visually striking.
- Adjust saturation levels to enhance the color without making it look unnatural.

Color Grading Techniques

- Use LUTs (Lookup Tables) to apply specific color styles.
- Create a warm tone for unboxings and hardware reviews.
- Use a cool tone for software tutorials to create a professional, clean look.

Optimizing Video Length

YouTube favors videos with higher watch times, so optimizing the length is essential. Most successful tech videos are between 8 to 12 minutes long. However, for complex tutorials or product reviews, longer videos (15 to 20 minutes) are acceptable if the content remains engaging.

Recommended Video Export Settings

Setting	Recommended Value
Resolution	1080p (1920 × 1080) or 4K (3840 × 2160)
Frame Rate	30 fps or 60 fps
Codec	H.264
Bitrate	8,000 – 12,000 Kbps (1080p)
Audio Format	AAC
Audio Bitrate	192 Kbps

Mastering the editing and post-production process allows you to transform raw footage into a polished, professional video that attracts and retains viewers. By cutting and trimming footage, enhancing audio, adding effects, and optimizing color, you create a cohesive and engaging viewing experience. High-quality editing increases audience retention, boosts channel credibility, and improves YouTube rankings — setting the foundation for long-term success.

Chapter 8

Creating Eye-Catching Thumbnails and Titles

Creating high-quality tech videos is only part of the equation for success on YouTube. The other equally critical component is ensuring that potential viewers click on your videos in the first place. No matter how valuable or well-produced a video is, it won't generate views or engagement if people aren't compelled to click on it. This is where thumbnails and titles play a pivotal role. Thumbnails and titles serve as the first impression of a video, acting as the gateway between content and the audience.

Thumbnails and titles are the primary drivers of click-through rates (CTR), which is one of the most important metrics in YouTube's algorithm. A high CTR signals to YouTube that a video is appealing to viewers, prompting the algorithm to recommend it to more users. This creates a positive feedback loop where a high CTR leads to increased exposure, which in turn increases views, watch time, and subscriber growth.

A compelling thumbnail grabs attention instantly, even when surrounded by competing content. It needs to convey the video's content visually while sparking curiosity or excitement. A well-crafted title complements the thumbnail by reinforcing the video's value proposition and providing context. Together, the thumbnail and title form a powerful combination that determines whether a potential viewer will engage with the video or scroll past it.

This chapter explores the techniques for creating visually appealing thumbnails using popular design tools, the strategies for writing click-worthy yet honest titles, and the psychological triggers that increase the likelihood of viewers clicking on your content. Mastering these techniques ensures that your videos stand out in a crowded platform, driving more views and increasing overall channel growth.

Thumbnails and Titles in Driving Clicks

YouTube's recommendation algorithm is heavily influenced by user engagement signals, including watch time, likes, comments, and, most importantly, click-through rates (CTR). A high CTR indicates that users are drawn to the video's presentation, which prompts the algorithm to suggest the video to more viewers. Conversely, a low CTR can limit the video's reach, even if the content itself is valuable.

Thumbnails and titles are the first elements that viewers see when browsing YouTube's search results or recommended videos. The human brain processes visual information 60,000 times faster than text, making the thumbnail the primary driver of the initial decision to click. However, the title reinforces the thumbnail's message and provides the necessary context to encourage engagement.

A well-designed thumbnail paired with a clear and intriguing title can improve a video's CTR by up to **20-30%**. This increase in CTR translates into higher views, longer watch times, and increased channel authority — all of which contribute to long-term growth.

Impact of CTR on Video Performance

CTR (%)	Expected Outcome
Below 2%	Poor performance; video unlikely to gain traction
2% - 5%	Average performance; moderate organic reach
5% - 10%	High performance; algorithm likely to promote the video
Above 10%	Excellent performance; high organic reach and growth potential

Thumbnails and titles work together to capture attention and influence the viewer's decision-making process. While the thumbnail triggers emotional engagement through visuals, the title provides the logical context that convinces the viewer that the video is worth watching.

Designing Eye-Catching Thumbnails

A thumbnail should be visually appealing, easy to understand at a glance, and relevant to the video content. The goal is to make the thumbnail stand out in a sea of competing videos while accurately reflecting the video's value.

Key Elements of an Effective Thumbnail

High-Resolution Image – The thumbnail should have a resolution of **1280 x 720 pixels** or higher, ensuring that it appears sharp on all devices.

Bold, Readable Text – Adding text to a thumbnail helps clarify the video's topic. The text should be large enough to be readable on small screens and limited to **three to five words** for clarity.

Contrasting Colors – High contrast between the text and background ensures that the thumbnail is readable and visually striking.

Emotional Faces and Expressions – Human faces with exaggerated expressions (such as surprise, excitement, or confusion) tend to draw more attention.

Visual Focus – The thumbnail should have a single point of focus, such as a product, software interface, or person's face, to avoid visual clutter.

Branding Elements – Including the channel logo or consistent color scheme reinforces brand recognition and helps viewers associate the video with your channel.

Guide for Creating Thumbnails Using Canva

Open Canva and select a custom canvas size of **1280 x 720 pixels**.

Upload the video's key frame or a high-quality still image related to the content.

Add bold, readable text using a font that contrasts well with the background. Limit the text to essential words, such as "Best Tech Tips" or "Unboxing Review."

Apply a high-contrast color scheme. Bright colors like yellow, red, and green tend to perform well on YouTube.

Include a human face with a strong expression if relevant to the content. Studies show that thumbnails with human faces tend to achieve **30% higher CTR**.

Export the thumbnail in PNG format to maintain high resolution and clarity.

Examples of Successful Thumbnails

Thumbnail Type	Example Description	CTR Impact
Product Close-Up	High-quality image of a smartphone with large text "Best Camera Test"	+15% CTR
Face + Emotion	Person holding a product with a surprised expression	+20% CTR
Clean and Minimal	Simple software interface with bold text "How to Fix It"	+10% CTR

Writing Click-Worthy Titles

While thumbnails drive emotional engagement, titles provide logical context and persuade viewers to click. A strong title should be clear, engaging, and aligned with the video's content.

Best Practices for Crafting Titles

Keep it Under 60 Characters – Shorter titles are more readable and less likely to be cut off in search results.

Use Power Words – Words like "Best," "Top," "Easy," and "Fast" tend to increase CTR by creating a sense of value or urgency.

Create Curiosity – Phrasing the title as a question or mystery can increase curiosity and encourage clicks.

Include Keywords – Relevant keywords help the video rank higher in search results. Placing the main keyword at the beginning of the title increases visibility.

Avoid Clickbait – Misleading titles can lead to high bounce rates, which negatively affect video rankings.

Examples of Effective Titles

Title Type	Example	CTR Impact
How-To	"How to Fix a Slow Laptop in 5 Minutes"	+20% CTR
Listicle	"Top 10 Free Video Editing Tools for 2025"	+15% CTR
Curiosity	"You Won't Believe What This Smartphone Can Do!"	+18% CTR
Product Review	"iPhone 15 Review – Is It Worth the Hype?"	+12% CTR

Triggers Behind Successful Titles

Curiosity and FOMO (Fear of Missing Out) are two powerful psychological triggers that increase click rates. Titles that pose a question or hint at a surprising outcome create an information gap that viewers feel compelled to close by clicking. Additionally, incorporating numbers or time-based language ("in 5 minutes") creates a sense of specificity and value, increasing the perceived usefulness of the video.

Thumbnails and titles are critical to driving engagement and growth on YouTube. A visually appealing thumbnail captures attention, while a well-crafted title reinforces the viewer's decision to click. By following best practices for design and language, you can create an irresistible combination that increases click-through rates, enhances video performance, and accelerates channel growth. Investing time and effort into creating strong thumbnails and titles is one of the highest-impact strategies for improving your video's visibility and overall success.

Chapter 9

Uploading and Optimizing Videos for SEO

Creating a high-quality tech video is only the beginning of building a successful YouTube channel. Once the video is filmed, edited, and polished, the next critical step is uploading and optimizing it for YouTube's search algorithm. Optimization ensures that your video is discoverable by both search engines and YouTube's internal recommendation system. Without proper search engine optimization (SEO), even the most well-crafted video can struggle to gain traction.

SEO on YouTube revolves around metadata, which includes the video's title, description, tags, and hashtags. When viewers search for content or browse suggested videos, YouTube's algorithm relies on this metadata to match the viewer's search intent with the most relevant videos. Therefore, correctly optimizing your video's metadata increases its chances of appearing in search results, suggested videos, and the "up next" section.

Beyond metadata, YouTube's algorithm also considers user engagement metrics such as watch time, click-through rate (CTR), likes, comments, and shares. Optimizing these engagement signals involves using features like timestamps, chapters, cards, and end screens to keep viewers watching and interacting with the content. Increasing watch time and engagement improves the video's ranking in search results and strengthens the channel's overall authority.

This chapter provides a comprehensive, step-by-step guide on uploading and optimizing tech videos for YouTube. It explores techniques for writing engaging titles and descriptions, selecting relevant tags and hashtags, creating useful timestamps and chapters, and using cards and end screens to boost engagement. By following these strategies, you can increase your video's visibility, attract more viewers, and grow your channel consistently.

Guide for Uploading a Video to YouTube

Uploading a video to YouTube is a straightforward process, but optimizing it for maximum visibility requires attention to detail at each step. Here is a step-by-step guide to uploading and optimizing a video-

Log into YouTube Studio – Open YouTube and navigate to the YouTube Studio dashboard.

Click on "Create" – Select the "Create" button in the top-right corner of the screen and choose "Upload Video."

Select the Video File – Choose the video file from your device. Ensure that the file is in one of YouTube's supported formats, such as MP4, MOV, or AVI.

Add Video Details – Once the upload begins, YouTube will prompt you to add the video's metadata, including the title, description, tags, and thumbnail. This is where SEO optimization starts.

Set Audience and Privacy Settings – Indicate whether the video is intended for children and select the appropriate privacy settings (public, private, or unlisted).

Add Advanced Settings – Add subtitles, captions, and recording location, and choose the video category to improve search relevance.

Save and Publish – Once all details are added, click "Publish" to make the video live or schedule it for a future release.

Writing Effective Titles and Descriptions

Crafting an Optimized Title

The video title is the most important piece of metadata because it directly influences whether viewers click on the video. The title should be clear, concise, and keyword-rich while sparking curiosity or interest. Ideally, the title should be no longer than **60 characters** to prevent it from being truncated in search results.

Using a combination of primary and secondary keywords increases the chances of the video appearing in search results. For example, if the video is about building a gaming PC, a good title could be-

"How to Build a Gaming PC Under $1000 – Step-by-Step Guide"

This title includes both the primary keyword "Build a Gaming PC" and secondary keywords like "Under $1000" and "Step-by-Step Guide," improving the video's relevance in search results.

Writing a Strong Description

The video description provides additional context for YouTube's algorithm and viewers. It should summarize the video's content, include relevant keywords, and provide useful links or timestamps. YouTube indexes the first **150 characters** of the description, making them crucial for SEO. A well-optimized description might look like this-

"In this video, I'll show you how to build a high-performance gaming PC for under $1000. Learn how to choose the right components, assemble them step-by-step, and optimize your system for the best gaming experience. Watch until the end for bonus tips on maximizing FPS!"

The description should also include links to relevant resources, such as affiliate links for the products mentioned in the video or links to related videos on your channel.

Adding Relevant Tags and Hashtags

Tags and hashtags help YouTube's algorithm understand the video's topic and recommend it to the right audience. While YouTube's algorithm places less importance on tags than on titles and descriptions, using the right tags can improve search ranking.

Best Practices for Adding Tags

Use a mix of broad and specific tags to cover different search intents. For example, a video about building a gaming PC could include both "Gaming PC" (broad) and "Build Gaming PC Under 1000" (specific).

Include related terms and synonyms to capture variations in search queries.

Add branded tags, such as your channel name or series name, to improve visibility within your own content network.

Using Hashtags

Hashtags are clickable and allow viewers to discover related content. They should be included at the end of the description or in the title itself. For example, using

#GamingPC or #TechTips allows the video to appear in hashtag-based search results.

Using Timestamps and Chapters

Timestamps and chapters improve user experience and engagement by allowing viewers to navigate the video more easily. Adding timestamps creates clickable sections in the video's progress bar, which encourages viewers to jump to the parts that interest them most.

To add timestamps, include them in the video description like this-

Timestamp	Section Name
00-00	Introduction
02-30	Choosing Components
05-15	Assembling the PC
12-45	BIOS Setup and Optimization
18-30	Bonus Tips

YouTube will automatically convert these timestamps into clickable chapters, improving viewer retention and satisfaction.

Adding Cards and End Screens

Cards and end screens help drive traffic to other videos on your channel, increasing overall watch time and session duration — two key factors in YouTube's recommendation algorithm.

Cards

Cards appear as small pop-ups during the video, encouraging viewers to watch related content or visit an external link. Best practices include placing cards at strategic points in the video when viewers are likely to drop off or need additional context.

End Screens

End screens appear during the last 5–20 seconds of a video and can include clickable links to other videos, playlists, or subscription buttons. Creating a consistent end screen design strengthens channel branding and encourages viewers to stay within your content ecosystem.

Discoverability Through YouTube Search

YouTube's search algorithm considers both metadata (title, description, tags) and user engagement (watch time, likes, comments) to rank videos. Increasing engagement through calls to action ("like, comment, and subscribe") boosts a video's ranking potential.

Suggested videos are based on YouTube's recommendation engine, which favors videos with high watch time and session duration. Creating playlists and linking related content in the description increases the chances of your videos appearing in the "Up Next" and "Suggested Videos" sections.

Uploading and optimizing tech videos for SEO is essential for maximizing their visibility and reach. Crafting compelling titles and descriptions, adding targeted tags and hashtags, and using timestamps, chapters, cards, and end screens increase a video's discoverability and engagement. High click-through rates and watch times signal to YouTube's algorithm that your content is valuable, leading to increased exposure and consistent channel growth. By mastering the techniques outlined in this chapter, you can significantly enhance your video's performance and establish a strong presence in the competitive tech content niche.

Chapter 10

Building an Engaged Community

Creating high-quality tech content is only one part of the equation for success on YouTube. The other crucial element is building and nurturing a strong, engaged community. Your viewers are the backbone of your channel, and maintaining active engagement with them will lead to increased loyalty, more interactions, and ultimately a stronger presence on the platform. This chapter explores the importance of community-building in the growth of your channel and outlines practical steps you can take to foster an interactive and supportive environment for your audience.

A thriving community on YouTube doesn't just happen automatically; it requires intentional strategies to keep your viewers involved and invested in your content. Engaging with your audience creates a sense of belonging, encourages repeat views, and increases the likelihood that viewers will share your videos, recommend your channel, and even become ambassadors for your brand. At the same time, having a loyal community boosts your visibility on YouTube's recommendation algorithms, increasing the chances that your videos will be shown to more viewers.

The Power of the Comment Section

The comment section is one of the most direct ways to interact with your audience. It provides a platform for viewers to express their thoughts, share their experiences, and ask questions. By responding to comments, you demonstrate that you value the feedback of your viewers and encourage further interaction.

When you reply to comments, it's essential to personalize your responses. A generic "Thanks for watching!" might not be enough to build a meaningful connection. Instead, take the time to address specific points raised in the comment. For example, if a viewer asks for further clarification on a technical aspect of a tutorial, provide a detailed response or even suggest additional resources that could help. By engaging in this way, you foster an environment where viewers feel heard, appreciated, and more likely to return.

In addition to replying to comments, you should also encourage your viewers to leave feedback and questions. This can be done through the video itself, where you explicitly ask for comments, or through the video description where you prompt viewers to engage. Asking open-ended questions such as, "What are your thoughts on this product?" or "Do you agree with my analysis of this tech trend?" can stimulate conversation and boost comment activity.

Live Streaming for Real-Time Interaction

Live streaming offers a unique opportunity to engage with your audience in real-time. It allows you to answer questions, provide insights, and build a deeper connection with your viewers. Live streams are particularly powerful for tech creators, as they provide an opportunity for on-the-spot demonstrations, Q&A sessions, and real-time troubleshooting.

Live streaming also creates a sense of urgency, as viewers can interact with you in real-time, something they cannot do with pre-recorded videos. The instant gratification of getting responses to their questions or comments creates a bond between you and your viewers. In addition, YouTube's algorithm favors live streams by promoting them in the notifications of your subscribers, which can help you grow your audience and increase live viewership.

For live streaming to be effective, it's important to plan ahead. Promote your upcoming live stream in advance, so your audience knows when to expect it. You should also prepare a general outline or topic for the stream to ensure it stays focused and engaging. Respond to viewers' comments as they come in, creating a dynamic back-and-forth exchange, and consider incorporating interactive elements, such as live polls or live technical demonstrations, to keep the energy high and viewers involved.

Using Community Posts

YouTube offers a feature called "Community Posts," which is an underutilized tool for channel owners to interact with their audience outside of video uploads. Community Posts can be used for a wide variety of purposes, including polls, text updates, photos, and links. This tool allows you to keep your audience engaged between video uploads and provide them with a more personal, direct connection with your channel.

Polls are particularly effective in building interaction. You can use polls to ask your audience about their preferences, thoughts on upcoming content, or their opinions on a particular topic. For example, if you're planning a tech tutorial on building a custom PC, you could run a poll asking viewers what components they would like to learn about in more detail. This not only provides valuable feedback but also gives your audience a sense of ownership over the content you create.

Community Posts also allow you to share behind-the-scenes glimpses of your creative process, ask for feedback on video topics, or provide updates on your channel's schedule. You can even use them to thank your viewers or acknowledge milestones, further strengthening the bond with your community.

Responding to Feedback

One of the most important aspects of building a community is responding to feedback. Whether it's positive or critical, feedback helps you understand what your audience values and where you can improve. Constructive criticism is invaluable in guiding your content creation, and responding thoughtfully to it shows that you are open to growth.

When viewers leave feedback, whether it's a compliment, a question, or a suggestion, taking the time to respond meaningfully is key. When responding to positive comments, express gratitude and acknowledge their support. This helps to encourage more positive interaction, as viewers are likely to appreciate your kindness and will return to engage again.

On the other hand, responding to critical feedback is equally important. Sometimes, viewers may point out mistakes or areas where you could improve. Instead of brushing off negative comments, take the opportunity to engage in a constructive conversation. This shows that you're not only interested in making great content but also in learning and growing from your audience's perspectives. If you made a mistake in a tutorial, for example, acknowledging it and offering a clarification shows that you value accuracy and are committed to improving.

Building relationships goes beyond simply replying to comments. You can further engage with your viewers by creating a sense of exclusivity. For instance, consider using YouTube's membership feature to offer exclusive content or perks to your most dedicated viewers. These viewers may appreciate the opportunity to access early content, behind-the-scenes footage, or direct communication with you.

Encouraging User Interaction

A large, engaged subscriber base is a hallmark of a successful channel. Subscribers are more likely to interact with your content and return to your channel regularly, making them vital to your channel's growth. Encouraging user interaction is the key to fostering loyalty and ensuring that viewers don't just watch once but subscribe and come back for more.

One effective strategy for building a subscriber base is to provide a strong call to action (CTA) in each of your videos. Ask viewers to subscribe and explain why it would benefit them. Instead of simply saying, "Don't forget to subscribe," you might say something like, "If you want more in-depth tech tutorials, don't forget to hit the subscribe button so you never miss a video!" This creates an additional incentive for viewers to subscribe and ensures that they understand the value your channel provides.

Another effective tactic is to create series-based content or offer exclusive content for subscribers. When viewers know that subscribing to your channel will give them access to ongoing content (such as a weekly series), they are more likely to subscribe to keep up with new episodes.

Creating interactive content such as polls, quizzes, or viewer challenges can also increase interaction and incentivize viewers to subscribe. For example, you might create a series of "tech challenges" where viewers are encouraged to follow along and comment on their results. This encourages repeat visits and builds a stronger community around your channel.

Finally, always take the time to express gratitude for your subscribers. Recognizing milestones such as hitting subscriber count goals or thanking viewers for supporting the channel creates a positive, community-oriented environment. You can do this in videos, community posts, or even by giving shout-outs to active subscribers in your content.

Building an engaged community is essential for sustaining long-term success on YouTube. By actively engaging with your audience through comments, live streams, and community posts, you create a space where viewers feel valued and heard. Responding to feedback, both positive and negative, helps foster relationships, allowing you to grow and improve alongside your audience. Encouraging user interaction, whether through strong calls to action or creating interactive content, ensures that viewers stay engaged and subscribed to your channel. A loyal, engaged community will not only help your channel grow but will also provide invaluable support, ensuring that your content reaches the right people and continues to thrive.

Chapter 11

Growing Your Channel with Analytics and Feedback

As a YouTube content creator, understanding your channel's performance and making data-driven decisions is essential for sustained growth and success. While creating high-quality content is undoubtedly important, being able to assess how well your videos are resonating with your audience is equally critical. In this chapter, we will explore how to leverage YouTube Studio to analyze your channel's performance. By learning how to use YouTube's built-in analytics tools effectively, you can make informed decisions about what's working, what's not, and how to adjust your content strategy for optimal growth.

Watch Time

Watch time is one of the most important metrics to track when evaluating the success of your YouTube videos. This metric refers to the total amount of time that viewers spend watching your content. Watch time is significant because YouTube's algorithm heavily favors videos with higher watch time, as it indicates that viewers are engaging with and enjoying the content.

Watch time is a reflection of how well your content holds viewers' attention. A high watch time suggests that your videos are compelling, informative, or entertaining enough to keep people watching until the end. On the other hand, low watch time might indicate that your videos are not engaging enough, or that the pacing, content structure, or quality might need improvement.

To check watch time in YouTube Studio, navigate to the "Analytics" tab and select "Watch time." Here, you'll see the total watch time for your videos, both in terms of hours and minutes. Tracking watch time over time will help you understand trends and identify which videos are performing well. A sharp drop in watch time after a certain point in a video could indicate that your content is losing viewer interest at that particular moment, prompting you to revisit your content structure or pacing.

Audience Retention

Audience retention is closely related to watch time but focuses specifically on how much of your video viewers watch before they click away. It's essentially a measurement of how long people stay engaged with your content. This metric is valuable because it can pinpoint specific points in your video where viewers are losing interest.

A good retention rate typically means that your content is capturing and maintaining the attention of your audience. If you see that viewers drop off at certain moments of the video, such as early on or toward the end, it might signal that your introduction is too long or that the content becomes less interesting as the video progresses. Adjusting your content based on audience retention can significantly improve your videos' performance.

YouTube provides a graph in the analytics section of your channel that shows audience retention for each video. You can compare retention rates across videos and track how changes to your video style or format influence this metric.

Click-Through Rate (CTR)

Click-through rate (CTR) is a metric that tells you how effective your video's thumbnail and title are at attracting clicks. It's calculated by dividing the number of clicks your video receives by the number of impressions it gets. The higher the CTR, the better your thumbnail and title are at convincing viewers to click on your video.

CTR is crucial because it reflects how well you're capturing your audience's attention in a sea of content. A low CTR might indicate that your thumbnails or titles are not compelling enough or that they are not aligned with your video's content. Improving CTR can significantly increase the number of views on your videos, leading to higher growth and visibility on YouTube.

To analyze CTR in YouTube Studio, go to the "Reach" section under Analytics, where you'll find data on impressions and the corresponding CTR. If you notice a low CTR, consider tweaking your thumbnails or titles by making them more visually appealing, ensuring they accurately reflect your content, or testing different variations to see what resonates best with your audience.

Identifying High-Performing Content

One of the most powerful features of YouTube's analytics is its ability to show which content resonates most with your audience. By identifying high-performing videos, you can gain insights into what topics, formats, or styles are most popular with your viewers. This information can help you focus your efforts on content that is most likely to succeed, rather than wasting time on videos that may not perform well.

In YouTube Studio, you can view your top-performing videos by selecting the "Top videos" tab in the "Analytics" section. This will show you the videos that have received the most views, watch time, and engagement. By analyzing these videos, you can identify patterns that may explain their success.

For instance, if a particular video about a product review has received significantly higher views and engagement than other videos on your channel, it could indicate that there is strong interest in that product or category. This might suggest that you should create similar content, such as reviews of related products, tutorials, or comparisons. Conversely, if your tutorials tend to perform better than unboxing videos, you might consider shifting your focus toward creating more educational content for your audience.

High-performing content can also help you determine which topics are most in demand. Use this information to refine your content strategy, ensuring you create videos that align with what your audience wants to see.

Understanding Audience Demographics

YouTube provides detailed insights into the demographics of your audience, which can be incredibly helpful for tailoring your content to your viewers' interests. By analyzing demographic data such as age, gender, location, and viewing devices, you can create content that speaks directly to the needs and preferences of your audience.

In the "Audience" section of YouTube Studio, you can view the demographic breakdown of your viewers. For example, you may find that a significant portion of your audience consists of viewers aged 18-34, or that your content is particularly popular in specific countries. Understanding these patterns allows you to refine your content and make it more relevant to your audience's interests.

Knowing where your audience is located geographically can also influence your video content and publishing schedule. For instance, if you have a large audience in the United States, it may be beneficial to post content during peak viewing times in that region, increasing the likelihood that your videos will be seen by a wider audience.

Similarly, analyzing the devices your audience uses to watch your videos (e.g., mobile phones, tablets, or desktop computers) can help you optimize your videos for those specific platforms. For example, if a majority of your viewers watch on mobile devices, you may want to ensure that your thumbnails, text, and visuals are optimized for smaller screens.

Adjusting Content Strategy Based on Analytics

Once you have gathered enough data, it's time to use that information to make informed decisions about your content strategy. YouTube analytics provides a wealth of data that can guide your content creation process, helping you prioritize topics, formats, and styles that resonate with your audience.

If your analytics show that certain types of videos (e.g., tutorials, reviews, or tech news updates) consistently perform well, consider producing more content in those categories. If you notice that certain video lengths or formats have higher retention rates, use that data to adjust how long your videos are or how you present your content.

You can also adjust your upload frequency based on audience behavior. If you find that your audience is more engaged with videos uploaded on weekends, for example, you may want to plan your content schedule accordingly.

Regularly reviewing your YouTube analytics will help you stay on top of changing trends and evolving viewer preferences. Use these insights to refine your content strategy continuously, ensuring that your channel stays fresh and relevant.

In summary, using YouTube Studio's analytics tools is crucial for growing your channel and making data-driven decisions. By analyzing metrics such as watch time, audience retention, CTR, and demographics, you can better understand your audience's preferences and make adjustments to improve engagement. Identifying high-performing content will help you create more of what your viewers want, while understanding your audience's demographics allows you to tailor your content to their interests and needs. Ultimately, regularly assessing and adjusting your content strategy based on analytics is key to achieving long-term growth on YouTube.

Chapter 12

Collaborations and Networking

As a YouTube content creator, particularly in the tech niche, one of the most effective ways to accelerate your channel's growth is through collaborations and networking. While producing high-quality content is essential for building a loyal audience, collaborations allow you to tap into new audiences, gain fresh perspectives, and enhance your channel's credibility. This chapter will explore the powerful role that collaborations play in YouTube growth, guide you through the process of partnering with other creators, and offer strategies for using networking to build a robust online presence.

Benefits of Collaborating with Other YouTubers

Collaborating with other content creators, especially within your niche, offers numerous advantages. One of the most immediate benefits of collaboration is the opportunity to expose your content to a broader audience. When you collaborate with a creator who already has an established audience, you have the chance to introduce your channel to viewers who may not have come across your content otherwise. This expanded visibility can lead to more subscribers, higher engagement, and, ultimately, more views on your videos.

Collaboration also provides the opportunity for cross-promotion, where both creators promote each other's content on their respective channels. This mutual promotion can help both parties gain new subscribers and build a stronger following. Furthermore, working with someone in the same niche ensures that your collaboration feels authentic and relevant to your audience. In the tech space, collaborations might involve co-hosting a product review, creating a joint DIY project, or discussing a trending tech topic, all of which appeal to both creators' audiences.

Another significant benefit of collaboration is the enhancement of your credibility and authority. Being featured alongside well-respected creators in the tech industry can help establish you as a trusted figure in your field. When you collaborate with creators who have already built a reputation, their endorsement acts as a form of social proof, which can lend credibility to your channel and content.

How to Approach Potential Collaborators

Finding the right collaborator is crucial. Ideally, you want to partner with someone whose content complements yours while sharing a similar target audience. In the tech niche, potential collaborators could be those who specialize in product reviews, unboxings, tutorials, DIY projects, or tech discussions, as these topics generally align with your audience's interests. Once you've identified a potential collaborator, it's important to approach them professionally and respectfully.

Start by researching the creator's content, engagement, and overall style to ensure they are a good fit for your channel. Familiarize yourself with their work and see if their audience overlaps with yours. Take note of their video production style, the type of tech content they focus on, and the audience engagement they receive.

When reaching out, make sure your pitch is clear and tailored to the specific creator. Introduce yourself and explain why you think a collaboration would be beneficial for both parties. Be specific about what you propose—whether it's a joint video, a series of collaborations, or simply promoting each other's content. Also, provide insight into the kind of value you bring to the table, such as your experience, unique ideas, or audience engagement metrics. It's crucial to show that you understand their work and that you've thought about how the collaboration would be mutually beneficial.

While crafting your approach, it's important to be polite, professional, and patient. Creators, especially those with larger audiences, are often inundated with collaboration requests. Take time to build a genuine relationship first, whether by commenting on their videos, engaging on social media, or sharing their content. This helps create rapport before formally reaching out. Keep your messages brief and to the point, and always remain respectful, even if you don't hear back right away.

Cross-Promoting Content

Cross-promotion is one of the most effective strategies for leveraging collaborations. By cross-promoting, both creators share each other's content to their respective audiences, driving more views, subscribers, and engagement. There are multiple ways to cross-promote content, and each approach provides value to both parties.

One common method is to collaborate on a single video, where both creators are featured. Once the video is live, both creators promote it on their channels, encouraging their subscribers to watch and engage. A tech collaboration could involve reviewing the same product from different angles or discussing a particular tech issue. For example, if you specialize in DIY electronics and a collaborator is known for product unboxing, you could team up to unbox a new tech gadget, showing both the unboxing and how to modify or upgrade it. This gives your audience a full picture of the product while introducing them to new content that appeals to their interests.

Another effective cross-promotion strategy is to feature one another on social media platforms. Sharing your collaboration video on platforms such as Instagram, Twitter, and Facebook, or even creating Instagram Stories, posts, and tweets about the collaboration, can help amplify your reach. You can also tag each other in the posts to ensure that both sets of followers are aware of the collaboration.

Collaborating on live streams is another great way to cross-promote. Live streams offer real-time interaction with your audience and can create a sense of urgency around your content. By inviting a collaborator to join you for a live session, you can reach a new audience and increase engagement. Live streams also encourage more interactive content, such as answering audience questions or discussing trending tech topics in real-time.

Leveraging Social Media Platforms for Growth

In addition to YouTube, social media platforms are powerful tools for growing your visibility and expanding your reach through collaborations. Platforms like Instagram, Twitter, LinkedIn, and Facebook provide a broader ecosystem where you can engage with audiences who may not be active on YouTube but still have an interest in tech content. Leveraging social media for networking and collaboration opportunities can be highly effective in attracting new subscribers to your channel.

One way to use social media for networking is by joining or participating in groups and communities related to your niche. Many tech-focused groups and forums exist on Facebook, Reddit, and even Discord, where you can interact with fellow creators and potential collaborators. These communities often provide a space for creators to share tips, ask questions, and discuss the latest trends, making it an ideal environment for establishing professional relationships.

Social media is also great for sharing behind-the-scenes content, announcements, and collaborations in real time. By promoting your YouTube collaborations on platforms like Twitter or Instagram, you can generate buzz and anticipation before the video drops. You can even host giveaways, polls, and Q&A sessions related to the collaboration to get your audience involved and excited.

By using these platforms strategically, you can not only cross-promote content but also find creators to collaborate with in the future. Engage with influencers and other content creators in your niche by liking, commenting, and sharing their posts. This helps build genuine connections that can eventually lead to collaboration opportunities.

Managing the Logistics of Collaborations

While collaborations can be incredibly rewarding, they also require careful planning and coordination. Once you've established a partnership, it's essential to discuss and outline the logistics of the collaboration. These details can include deciding on video topics, agreeing on deadlines, and determining how the content will be promoted across both creators' channels.

When managing a collaboration, clear communication is key. Be sure to have a mutual understanding of expectations and responsibilities, including who will be responsible for shooting, editing, and promoting the video. It's also important to discuss any potential revenue-sharing arrangements if monetization is involved. If your collaboration includes sponsorships or affiliate marketing, make sure both parties are in agreement about how to handle these aspects to ensure transparency and fairness.

If the collaboration involves a product or brand, consider how each party will manage the sponsorship or product placement. Both creators should be aware of any contractual obligations, deadlines for promotions, and the key messaging for the product.

In conclusion, collaborations and networking are indispensable tools for growing a tech YouTube channel. By working with like-minded creators, you gain exposure to new audiences, strengthen your credibility, and create a richer variety of content. Approaching potential collaborators with a thoughtful, professional pitch, cross-promoting content, and leveraging social media platforms can exponentially increase your visibility. Additionally, managing the logistics of a collaboration with clear communication ensures a smooth and successful partnership. The tech industry thrives on collaboration, and by tapping into this network, you can elevate your channel to new heights, fostering growth, engagement, and long-term success.

Chapter 13

Monetizing Your Tech Channel

Monetizing a YouTube channel, particularly within the tech niche, offers a variety of opportunities to generate income from your hard work. Whether you're reviewing the latest tech products, creating tutorials, or discussing industry trends, there are numerous methods for turning your content into revenue. This chapter will explore different monetization strategies available to YouTubers, such as the YouTube Partner Program, affiliate marketing, sponsored videos, selling merchandise, and crowdfunding. Moreover, it will provide a comprehensive overview of how to maximize your income while maintaining audience trust and integrity.

YouTube Partner Program (YPP)

The YouTube Partner Program (YPP) is one of the most direct ways to monetize your channel, offering creators the opportunity to earn revenue through ads shown on their videos. The process of qualifying for the program involves meeting certain criteria set by YouTube, such as having a minimum of 1,000 subscribers and 4,000 watch hours within the last 12 months. Additionally, your channel must comply with YouTube's policies and community guidelines, and you need to have a linked AdSense account.

Once accepted into the YouTube Partner Program, you can start earning revenue through various types of ads, including display ads, overlay ads, skippable and non-skippable video ads, and bumper ads. The amount you earn depends on several factors, including your audience's location, the content of your videos, and the type of ad displayed. Advertisers pay based on Cost Per Thousand Impressions (CPM), meaning you earn money for every 1,000 views on an ad displayed on your video.

The CPM varies widely in the tech niche depending on the specific type of content and the demographic of your audience. For example, tech channels that focus on high-ticket items like smartphones, laptops, and gadgets might have a higher CPM because tech products typically attract higher-paying advertisers. In contrast, general tech discussions or lower-cost tech products might bring in a lower CPM. Therefore, understanding your audience's demographic—such as their location, interests, and buying behavior—is critical in optimizing your ad revenue.

While YouTube ad revenue can be a steady income stream, it may not be the most lucrative option for every creator. CPM rates fluctuate depending on seasonal demand, advertiser budgets, and even the global economic situation. As such, many creators turn to supplemental monetization strategies to further maximize their income.

Affiliate Marketing

Affiliate marketing is one of the most popular and profitable ways for tech YouTubers to monetize their content. By promoting products or services from external companies, you can earn a commission on any sales generated through your unique referral links. Affiliate marketing works particularly well in the tech niche, where product recommendations and reviews are common.

One of the most well-known affiliate programs is Amazon Associates. Through this program, YouTubers can link to products sold on Amazon, earning a percentage of the sale price when viewers make purchases through the provided links. The advantage of Amazon's affiliate program is its extensive product catalog, making it suitable for almost any type of tech content. Whether you're reviewing smartphones, laptops, software, or accessories, you can easily find affiliate products to promote.

Another option for tech creators is partnering directly with tech brands or services that offer affiliate commissions. Many tech companies, ranging from software companies like Adobe and Microsoft to hardware providers like Logitech or Razer, offer affiliate programs where creators can earn commissions on sales of their products. These affiliate programs often offer higher commissions than Amazon Associates, especially for higher-end products or services.

To effectively use affiliate marketing, it's important to be transparent with your audience about your affiliations. Ethical affiliate marketing ensures that you only recommend products that align with your values and that you believe will genuinely benefit your viewers. Providing honest, detailed reviews of products and showcasing how they work in your tech projects will build trust with your audience, making them more likely to use your affiliate links.

It's also worth noting that affiliate marketing isn't limited to physical products. You can also promote software, online tools, or services, many of which offer recurring commissions for subscriptions. For example, you could promote cloud storage services, tech courses, or productivity tools, which are highly relevant to your audience and provide steady income over time.

Sponsored Videos and Product Reviews

Sponsored videos are another popular monetization method, especially within the tech industry. Brands will pay YouTubers to create content featuring their products or services. This can be in the form of product reviews, tutorials, unboxings, or even full-length videos discussing the benefits of a particular tech solution. Sponsored content can be a highly lucrative income source, particularly for channels with a strong, engaged audience.

Sponsorships often involve negotiating a fixed fee with the brand or company. The amount of money a brand is willing to pay depends on factors like your channel's size, audience engagement, and niche relevance. Typically, larger channels with millions of subscribers will command higher fees, but even smaller creators can earn substantial amounts from sponsorships if they have a highly engaged and targeted audience.

When accepting sponsored content, it's crucial to maintain transparency with your viewers. Always disclose sponsorships clearly by following YouTube's guidelines and including statements such as "This video is sponsored by [Brand]" in the video description and during the video itself. This transparency builds trust and ensures that your audience knows when content is sponsored.

Additionally, you can create sponsored videos by offering an honest, unbiased review of a product. Many companies in the tech space rely on video reviews to boost their product visibility, but it's important to approach sponsored reviews with integrity. Provide honest feedback, even if the product has flaws. Your audience will respect you more for giving them the full picture, and brands that value genuine feedback will be more inclined to work with you long-term.

Selling Merchandise and Memberships

Selling merchandise is an increasingly popular method of monetization for YouTubers. As a tech creator, you can sell branded merchandise like t-shirts, hats, mugs, or posters featuring your logo or catchy phrases related to your channel. Platforms such as Teespring, Spreadshop, and Printful offer print-on-demand services, allowing you to create and sell custom merchandise without upfront costs. The items are only produced when someone makes a purchase, meaning you don't need to worry about inventory or shipping logistics.

Another option is offering memberships through YouTube's own platform or external services. YouTube allows creators to set up channel memberships, where viewers can pay a monthly fee for access to exclusive content, badges, and live chats. These memberships can be a reliable source of income, particularly for tech channels that offer in-depth tutorials, behind-the-scenes content, or Q&A sessions. Additionally, platforms like Patreon and Buy Me a Coffee allow creators to offer exclusive content, perks, and direct interactions with their audience in exchange for financial support.

When selling merchandise or offering memberships, it's essential to provide value to your audience. Offer exclusive designs or unique products that resonate with your viewers. Consider releasing limited-edition items or special offers for your most loyal fans. This will not only generate revenue but also foster a sense of community and exclusivity.

Crowdfunding- Patreon and Buy Me a Coffee

Crowdfunding platforms, such as Patreon and Buy Me a Coffee, allow YouTubers to generate ongoing financial support directly from their audience. These platforms work on a subscription model where viewers can pledge a certain amount of money each month to support your channel. In return, supporters receive exclusive perks, such as access to bonus content, early video releases, or direct communication with the creator.

Patreon, for example, is widely used by creators to provide additional content such as in-depth tutorials, personal tech advice, and even one-on-one consultations. By offering these types of exclusive benefits, you can encourage your audience to contribute to your channel's growth. The key to success on platforms like Patreon is providing consistent value and maintaining a strong, loyal fanbase that is willing to financially support your work.

Buy Me a Coffee is another similar platform, but with a focus on one-time contributions, where viewers can donate money for individual videos, projects, or general support. This is ideal for creators who don't want to commit to long-term subscriptions but still want to receive occasional financial backing from their audience.

Crowdfunding is particularly effective for creators who have a dedicated fan base. It's important to build a community where your viewers feel invested in your content and are willing to support you financially in exchange for the added value you provide.

Maximizing Income While Maintaining Audience Trust

While the various monetization methods outlined above offer significant income opportunities, it's essential to balance revenue generation with maintaining your audience's trust. Transparency, authenticity, and consistency are key to ensuring that your monetization strategies align with your values and audience expectations.

First and foremost, always disclose any paid promotions, sponsorships, or affiliate links clearly and upfront. Transparency not only builds trust but also complies with YouTube's policies, which require creators to disclose paid content. If you're promoting products or services, be sure to only recommend those that align with your channel's ethos and are relevant to your audience's interests. A trusting audience will appreciate your integrity and be more likely to support your monetization efforts.

Additionally, avoid overwhelming your viewers with too many ads, affiliate links, or sponsorships in a single video. Instead, focus on providing high-quality, valuable content that engages and educates your audience. If your content is beneficial and engaging, your viewers will be more likely to support your monetization methods willingly, whether that's through subscribing, donating, or purchasing merchandise.

Monetizing your tech YouTube channel is an exciting and viable way to turn your passion for tech into a sustainable business. From ad revenue through the YouTube Partner Program to affiliate marketing, sponsored videos, selling merchandise, and crowdfunding, there are multiple strategies you can employ. However, it's crucial to approach monetization ethically, ensuring that you maintain your audience's trust while maximizing income. By carefully selecting the right monetization methods and being transparent with your audience, you can build a profitable channel that grows alongside your influence in the tech space.

Chapter 14

Advanced Growth Strategies

As a YouTuber in the tech space, you may already have mastered the fundamentals of video production, content optimization, and audience engagement. However, once you've laid a solid foundation, it becomes essential to adopt more advanced growth strategies to accelerate your channel's success and take it to the next level. This chapter explores a range of strategies that can help you increase your channel's visibility, grow your audience, and boost your overall performance. These advanced techniques include increasing watch time, creating viral content, leveraging trends, A/B testing thumbnails and titles, and investing in paid promotions.

Increasing Watch Time Through Playlists

Watch time is one of the most critical factors influencing your video's visibility on YouTube. The more time viewers spend watching your videos, the more likely YouTube's algorithm is to recommend your content to other users. One effective strategy for increasing watch time is creating playlists and designing binge-worthy content.

Playlists are a powerful tool for boosting watch time because they allow you to group related videos together, making it easy for viewers to watch multiple videos in a row without interruption. By creating well-structured playlists around specific topics or themes (such as "Beginner's Guide to Electronics" or "Top 10 Smartphone Reviews"), you can guide your audience through a series of videos that naturally encourage them to watch more of your content.

Binge-worthy content plays a key role in increasing watch time as well. To create this type of content, think of ways to keep viewers hooked and encourage them to continue watching. One technique is to design your videos to be part of a series. Each video should end with a teaser for the next video in the series, creating a sense of anticipation and curiosity. For example, if you're doing a product review series, mention in the last few moments of the video what's coming next, like "In the next video, we will take a deep dive into the battery performance of this phone, so don't miss it!" This encourages viewers to stay tuned and keep watching.

Furthermore, structuring your content to be long-form but valuable can also contribute to binge-watching habits. Longer videos (around 10 to 20 minutes) that dive deep into a subject tend to encourage viewers to keep watching, provided they are well-paced and engaging.

To fully take advantage of playlists, make sure your videos are organized with clear titles, tags, and descriptions that make them easy to find. You can also feature your playlists on your channel's homepage to help viewers discover more content. Playlists don't just help viewers watch more videos, they also signal to YouTube that people are engaging with your content, which can improve your ranking in search results and recommendations.

Creating Viral Content

Creating viral content is often seen as the Holy Grail of YouTube growth, but it's not as elusive as it may seem. While virality cannot always be predicted, there are certain principles that can significantly increase the likelihood of your content going viral.

The key to creating viral content lies in emotional connection. Videos that evoke strong emotional reactions—whether it's laughter, shock, excitement, or even nostalgia—tend to have higher engagement and shareability. In the tech space, viral content often revolves around major product launches, breakthrough innovations, or unique tech hacks that astonish viewers.

Incorporating elements that are highly shareable is another tactic. For instance, creating "reaction" or "comparison" videos where you analyze and react to a trending topic or a hot new product can quickly attract a large audience. These types of videos encourage viewers to share their thoughts in the comments, react on social media, and even share the video with others who are interested in the topic.

Another factor that can contribute to virality is timely content. Jumping on emerging trends or capitalizing on newsworthy events can increase your chances of going viral. For example, if there's a highly anticipated tech conference or a major tech product release, producing content about that event within hours of its conclusion can position your video to gain traction while the topic is fresh.

A great way to make your content viral-ready is to give it a compelling hook right from the start. The first few seconds of your video should grab attention immediately—whether that's through a bold statement, an intriguing question, or a surprising visual. Making your thumbnail and title irresistible is also key; they should make people want to click on your video instantly.

Though virality can't be guaranteed, creating compelling, emotionally engaging content around current trends or exciting product releases will certainly increase your chances.

Leveraging Trends and Seasonal Content

Trending topics and seasonal content offer great opportunities to grow your channel rapidly. By staying on top of the latest tech developments, global events, and popular themes, you can create content that resonates with your audience at the right moment.

In the tech industry, trends often include new product announcements, technology breakthroughs, and major company events like Apple or Google's annual conferences. Creating content around these events— such as live reactions, detailed analyses, or predictions—can put your videos in front of viewers who are eagerly searching for updates or insights on the topic.

Seasonal content is another area where you can capitalize on the rhythm of the year. For instance, during major shopping seasons like Black Friday, Cyber Monday, or the lead-up to Christmas, consumers are particularly interested in tech deals, product reviews, and gift guides. By producing content tailored to these times of the year, such as "Best Budget Laptops for Back-to-School" or "Top Tech Gifts for 2025," you increase the relevance of your videos to viewers who are actively shopping or looking for recommendations.

Incorporating trends and seasonal topics into your content strategy ensures that your videos remain timely and relevant, which increases the likelihood that they will be shared, searched for, and watched. If you can anticipate what will be trending, you can get ahead of the curve and position your content for success.

It's also helpful to stay updated on broader cultural trends outside of tech, such as shifts in lifestyle, environmental issues, or social media challenges. By tapping into popular themes that align with your tech focus, you can connect with a broader audience, making your channel even more appealing to potential subscribers.

A/B Testing Thumbnails and Titles

A/B testing is one of the most effective ways to optimize the discoverability and engagement of your videos. By experimenting with different versions of your thumbnails and titles, you can identify which ones resonate best with your audience and result in higher click-through rates (CTR).

The process of A/B testing involves creating two variations of a thumbnail or title and testing them on a small audience or in different periods of time to see which one performs better. For example, you might create two thumbnails- one with a close-up shot of a product and another featuring the product in use in a real-world setting. You could then compare the performance of each version to see which one attracts more clicks.

Similarly, titles can significantly impact your video's CTR. Titles should be compelling, concise, and optimized for search, but they should also stand out to potential viewers. Testing variations of titles—such as a straightforward "How-to" title versus one with a question or a sense of urgency—can reveal which phrasing engages your target audience more effectively.

Tools like TubeBuddy or VidIQ offer A/B testing features to streamline this process and provide detailed analytics. Once you've identified the best-performing version, you can apply the findings to all of your future videos, ensuring that your content is consistently optimized for maximum engagement.

Investing in Paid Promotions

While organic growth through YouTube's algorithms is ideal, investing in paid promotions can accelerate your channel's visibility, especially when you're aiming to reach a larger audience quickly. Paid promotions, through YouTube ads or social media ads, can significantly boost your channel's growth by putting your videos in front of a targeted audience.

YouTube offers several ad formats for creators to use, including skippable video ads, non-skippable video ads, bumper ads, and display ads. These ads can be targeted to specific audiences based on demographics, interests, and behaviors, making them highly effective for reaching viewers who are likely to engage with your content. For example, if you're running a tech channel focused on smartphone reviews, you can target your ads to people who have shown interest in mobile technology or electronics.

Paid promotions also extend beyond YouTube ads. Leveraging social media platforms like Facebook, Instagram, or Twitter can help boost your visibility and attract new subscribers. Ads on these platforms can be highly targeted based on user interests and online behavior, allowing you to reach potential viewers who are already interested in tech content.

Although investing in paid promotions can be costly, when done strategically, it can provide a strong return on investment (ROI) by growing your subscriber base quickly and increasing the reach of your videos. However, it's crucial to measure the effectiveness of your ad campaigns through analytics and adjust your strategy based on what's working and what isn't.

Advanced growth strategies are crucial to scaling your YouTube channel in a competitive environment. By focusing on increasing watch time, creating viral content, leveraging trends and seasonal content, A/B testing thumbnails and titles, and investing in paid promotions, you can accelerate your channel's growth and increase its reach. These strategies require careful planning and ongoing analysis to determine what works best for your unique audience and content style. As you implement these techniques, remember to stay true to your audience's interests, be transparent with them, and consistently deliver valuable content. By doing so, you'll not only grow your channel but also build a loyal community that supports you in the long term.

Chapter 15

Troubleshooting and Overcoming Challenges

As with any endeavor, running a YouTube channel comes with its fair share of challenges. These hurdles can range from dealing with negative feedback and copyright issues to combating creative burnout and continually improving your content's quality. The ability to effectively troubleshoot and navigate these obstacles will determine not only the success of your channel but also your personal resilience as a content creator. This chapter addresses the common problems faced by YouTubers, along with practical solutions and expert advice to help you overcome these setbacks.

Dealing with Negative Comments and Trolls

One of the most difficult aspects of being a content creator is facing negative comments, criticism, and trolls. Unfortunately, YouTube, like other social media platforms, attracts individuals who may leave unconstructive or hostile feedback, sometimes intentionally to provoke a reaction. These comments can be particularly challenging for new creators who may not yet have built up a thick skin or a strong support network. However, learning how to handle negativity effectively is crucial for your mental well-being and your channel's long-term growth.

The first step in dealing with negative comments is to recognize the difference between constructive criticism and trolling. Constructive criticism is usually specific, respectful, and offers useful suggestions on how to improve. It's important to view constructive criticism as an opportunity for growth. Responding with gratitude can show your audience that you are receptive to feedback and committed to improving. For instance, if a viewer suggests improving video sound quality, you might respond by saying, "Thanks for your feedback! I'll be working on enhancing the audio in future videos."

On the other hand, trolls are typically interested in provoking an emotional reaction rather than offering valid feedback. Trolls often use insults, profanity, or inflammatory remarks to undermine your confidence. In dealing with trolls, the best approach is usually to avoid engaging with them. Responding to their comments can fuel further negativity and escalate the situation. Instead, you can delete or block the commenter, and in some cases, report them to YouTube if they violate community guidelines. The focus should always be on maintaining a positive environment on your channel and not giving attention to individuals who try to disrupt it.

For creators who are overwhelmed by negative comments, taking breaks from reading comments can be helpful. Another strategy is to establish a positive feedback loop by actively seeking out and responding to supportive comments. By focusing more on the constructive and kind comments, you'll shift your perspective and reduce the impact of negativity.

Ultimately, remember that every YouTuber faces criticism, and it's a normal part of the journey. What matters most is how you respond to it and how you choose to learn from it or move past it.

Handling Copyright Claims and Strikes

As a tech creator, your content might often involve using music, images, video clips, or software that may be copyrighted. YouTube has a strict policy regarding copyrighted content, and violating it can lead to copyright claims or strikes. Understanding how to navigate these issues is essential to avoid potential setbacks that could hinder your channel's growth or even result in a suspension of your account.

A copyright claim occurs when the owner of copyrighted content identifies your use of their material. This is common when you use third-party media, such as music or video clips, without permission. In most cases, copyright owners do not seek to remove your video; instead, they may claim the revenue generated from the video, or in some instances, restrict access to certain regions. If you receive a copyright claim, you can either accept the claim or dispute it if you believe the use of the content falls under fair use. Fair use might include commentary, education, or criticism, but this is often a gray area, and YouTube encourages creators to carefully review the claims before deciding to dispute them.

A copyright strike is more severe than a claim. If you receive three copyright strikes on your channel, YouTube may terminate your account. Strikes usually happen when the copyright holder requests the removal of the video and takes further action against your account. The best way to avoid copyright strikes is to create original content and use copyright-free resources, such as Creative Commons-licensed music or royalty-free images. If you do use third-party content, always seek permission from the owner or use platforms like YouTube's Audio Library, which provides free music and sound effects for creators.

If you receive a strike, you'll have the opportunity to file a counter-notice if you believe the claim is erroneous. However, it's important to do this with caution, as filing false counter-notices can have legal consequences. To prevent future copyright issues, always give credit where it's due and use platforms that offer content with licenses suitable for commercial use.

Overcoming Creative Burnout

Creative burnout is a real and significant challenge that many content creators face, especially as they strive to maintain consistent video production and keep up with trends. The pressure to produce high-quality content on a regular basis can be overwhelming, leading to exhaustion and a lack of inspiration. Creative burnout can manifest in various ways- lack of motivation, difficulty coming up with new video ideas, or simply feeling like you're running on empty.

To combat creative burnout, the first step is recognizing the signs early on. If you're feeling drained, uninspired, or frustrated with the content creation process, it's crucial to take a step back and assess the situation. One practical solution is to give yourself a break. Taking a few days or even weeks off can help recharge your mental and creative energy. During this time, allow yourself to disconnect from the pressure of content production and focus on self-care. Engaging in hobbies or spending time with loved ones can help you reconnect with your passion for creating.

Another way to prevent burnout is to establish a sustainable production schedule. This might mean reducing the number of videos you upload per week or changing the format of your videos to something less time-consuming. Many creators find that batching content—filming multiple videos in one session—allows them to maintain consistency while avoiding the stress of last-minute content creation.

Collaborating with other creators can also provide a fresh perspective and a sense of camaraderie. Working with others not only brings new ideas into the creative process but can also relieve some of the pressure you may feel in doing everything alone. Networking within the creator community and exchanging ideas can help spark new inspiration and keep burnout at bay.

Lastly, always remember why you started your channel. Returning to the core purpose behind your content can reignite your passion and provide you with a clearer sense of direction. Whether your goal is to educate, entertain, or share your expertise, reconnecting with your 'why' can help you push through tough moments and continue producing content you're proud of.

Improving Content Quality Over Time

As a YouTuber, it's crucial to continuously strive for improvement in your content quality. This could involve enhancing video production elements, refining your delivery, or developing a more in-depth understanding of your audience's needs and preferences. Improving your content over time helps

159

maintain viewer interest, ensures long-term growth, and builds a loyal community.

One way to improve your content quality is by upgrading your equipment. As your channel grows, it's important to invest in better cameras, microphones, and lighting. The visual and audio quality of your videos is one of the first things viewers notice, and improving these elements can significantly enhance the professionalism of your content. For example, upgrading to a DSLR camera with a higher resolution, investing in an external microphone for clearer audio, and setting up proper lighting can dramatically elevate the overall quality of your videos.

Another key aspect of content improvement is refining your video editing skills. As you gain experience, you'll become more adept at using editing software to enhance your videos. Learning how to use advanced effects, transitions, color correction, and sound design will give your videos a polished, professional look. Taking courses or watching tutorials to hone your editing skills can help you stay competitive and continuously improve your content.

Don't forget about your storytelling. As you become more comfortable with the technical aspects of video production, focus on refining your narrative structure. Delivering your message in a clear, engaging, and authentic way is essential to keeping your audience's attention. Craft your content to flow smoothly from introduction to conclusion, and ensure that your delivery is enthusiastic and well-paced.

Finally, consistently analyzing your audience's feedback is one of the most effective ways to improve your content. Pay attention to comments, likes, dislikes, and audience retention data. If your audience provides suggestions for improvement, take them seriously and consider how you can incorporate their feedback into your future videos. Over time, this iterative process of listening to your audience and refining your approach will lead to greater success and higher content quality.

Every YouTuber will inevitably face setbacks, whether it's negative comments, copyright issues, burnout, or the ongoing challenge of improving content quality. The key to long-term success on the platform lies in how you handle these obstacles. By maintaining a positive mindset, using practical strategies to address challenges, and continually working to improve your content, you can overcome setbacks and thrive as a content creator. Always remember that problems are a natural part of the creative journey, and each one presents an opportunity to learn, adapt, and grow.

Chapter 16

Case Studies and Success Stories

In this chapter, we explore real-world examples of successful tech YouTubers, delving into their growth strategies, content styles, and monetization methods. By analyzing these case studies, we can uncover valuable lessons and actionable takeaways that aspiring YouTubers can apply to their own channels. Each story represents a unique journey, but there are common principles and strategies that all these creators have used to build successful tech channels, engage audiences, and turn their passion into profit.

Case Study 1- MKBHD – Marques Brownlee

Marques Brownlee, better known by his YouTube handle MKBHD, is one of the most well-known tech YouTubers, with over 16 million subscribers (as of 2025). His channel, which focuses primarily on technology reviews, product comparisons, and in-depth analysis, has become a go-to source for millions of viewers looking for reliable and thorough reviews of the latest gadgets, smartphones, and consumer electronics. Marques's success can be attributed to several key factors that aspiring tech YouTubers can learn from.

Growth Strategy- Consistency and Quality Content

MKBHD's success started with his commitment to producing high-quality content consistently. He initially gained attention with his smartphone reviews and tech tutorials, often using a minimalist, yet professional, presentation style. His clear focus on providing value—by making sure his audience understands both the features and limitations of the products he reviews—has played a significant role in building trust. His growth strategy is centered around consistency in video uploads, providing a steady stream of new content without sacrificing the quality of his work.

Another key element of his success is his dedication to constantly improving production quality. Early on, Marques was known for using professional-grade equipment, which helped his videos stand out in terms of clarity, sound, and visual appeal. Over time, he invested in more advanced tools, including high-definition cameras, sophisticated lighting setups, and professional audio equipment, to maintain a polished look for his videos. This investment paid off, allowing him to stand out in an increasingly competitive space.

Content Style- In-Depth Reviews and Analysis

MKBHD's content style revolves around delivering deep dives into the products he reviews. Rather than just providing surface-level opinions, he explains technical specifications in layman's terms while also addressing the real-world applications of the products. His reviews are well-researched and fact-based, with a clear emphasis on offering an honest evaluation. His credibility comes from his ability to explain complex technology concepts without overwhelming the viewer.

Marques has also established a signature style that resonates with his audience. His use of high-production visuals, clean editing, and crisp, straightforward narration ensures that his videos are both informative and engaging. His ability to simplify tech topics while maintaining accuracy has made him a trusted voice in the tech community.

Monetization Methods

As his channel grew, MKBHD began monetizing through multiple revenue streams. First and foremost, he leveraged YouTube's Partner Program, earning ad revenue from his videos. However, his true monetization success lies in diversifying his income sources. Through strategic brand partnerships, Marques has attracted lucrative sponsorship deals, often from the tech companies whose products he reviews. These partnerships help maintain his channel's sustainability while allowing him to provide unbiased reviews that his audience can trust.

In addition to sponsored content, Marques also uses affiliate marketing to monetize his content. He provides links to the products he reviews, and when his audience makes purchases through those links, he earns commissions. This method of monetization has allowed him to scale his revenue beyond traditional YouTube ad revenue.

Consistency in Content Creation- Regular uploads are key to growing a channel. Marques's ability to produce content consistently over the years has helped him maintain an engaged audience.

Invest in Quality- High-quality production equipment can significantly improve the appeal of your content. The better your video and audio quality, the more professional your channel will look, which builds trust.

Diversify Your Revenue Streams- Relying solely on ad revenue isn't sustainable in the long run. Building multiple revenue sources—through affiliate marketing, sponsorships, and partnerships—ensures greater financial stability.

Case Study 2- Linus Tech Tips – Linus Sebastian

Linus Tech Tips (LTT), founded by Linus Sebastian, is another highly successful tech channel with over 15 million subscribers. LTT is known for its comprehensive reviews, unboxings, and DIY computer builds. Linus's success on YouTube is primarily due to his innovative approach to content creation, his focus on entertainment, and his ability to build a strong brand identity.

Growth Strategy- Engaging and Entertaining Content

Linus initially gained popularity for his hands-on, fun approach to tech content. His content was both educational and entertaining, often including humorous skits, challenges, and over-the-top demonstrations. This style of content resonates well with his audience because it is not just about reviewing products—it's about creating an experience.

A major aspect of Linus's growth strategy is his team's ability to create viral content that blends informative reviews with humor. For example, videos that include tech "builds" or assembling custom computers are done in an engaging, high-energy format that makes complex topics fun. This approach helps capture the attention of a wider audience, particularly those who may not be avid tech enthusiasts but enjoy the entertaining nature of the content.

Mixing Education with Entertainment

Linus and his team have developed a content style that focuses on combining humor with technical knowledge. Their videos feature in-depth discussions of technology, yet they always incorporate an element of fun. For instance, in their DIY computer build series, Linus often invites team members to participate in challenges or funny skits that add personality to the content. This balance between education and entertainment helps LTT stand out in a crowded space by appealing to both tech enthusiasts and casual viewers alike.

The team also employs creative content formats, such as the "Techquickie" series, which provides concise explanations of various tech concepts. These bite-sized videos serve as a great way to break down complex topics in a short amount of time, appealing to viewers who prefer quick, informative content.

Sponsorships, Merchandising and YouTube Ad Revenue

Similar to MKBHD, Linus and his team at LTT have successfully diversified their revenue streams. Sponsorships play a significant role in their monetization strategy, with tech brands partnering with them for product placements and integrated marketing campaigns. LTT has also built its own merchandise line, which includes branded apparel and accessories. This has allowed them to further monetize their loyal audience while also creating an additional revenue stream.

Additionally, LTT benefits from YouTube ad revenue and affiliate marketing, although their emphasis on sponsored content and merchandise allows them to maximize earnings without relying solely on ads.

Entertainment is Key- Creating content that is both educational and entertaining will help you attract a broader audience. The more engaging your content is, the more likely it is to be shared and recommended by viewers.

Diversified Revenue Models- Building a sustainable income on YouTube requires more than just ad revenue. Focus on sponsorships, affiliate marketing, and merchandise sales to create a more stable revenue stream.

Branding and Identity- Developing a unique identity for your channel is crucial. By infusing your personality into your content, you can create a more relatable brand that resonates with viewers.

Case Study 3- Unbox Therapy – Lewis Hilsenteger

Unbox Therapy, run by Lewis Hilsenteger, is a tech channel with a focus on product unboxings, reviews, and first impressions. With over 17 million subscribers, the channel is one of the largest in the tech space. The success of Unbox Therapy can be attributed to its high-energy unboxing style, effective use of suspense, and strategic partnerships with tech companies.

Focused on Product Unboxing

One of the main factors behind Unbox Therapy's success is its specific focus on product unboxing. Lewis created a unique style of unboxing that was both engaging and informative. He doesn't just open boxes; he makes the experience exciting by revealing products in a suspenseful, cinematic way. This style has garnered a massive following, as viewers enjoy the thrill of discovering new tech through Lewis's enthusiastic and genuine reactions.

Additionally, Lewis has built strong relationships with tech companies, which ensures a constant stream of the latest products to unbox. This access to new products and technology has helped keep the channel fresh and relevant to its audience.

Suspenseful Unboxings and Engaging Reactions

Unbox Therapy's content style focuses heavily on suspense and genuine reactions. Lewis often emphasizes the "wow factor" of new products, using dramatic pauses and close-up shots to reveal the product in an exciting manner. His ability to connect with his audience through unfiltered excitement makes his unboxing videos both entertaining and educational. This sense of authenticity and enthusiasm is key to his success, as viewers feel like they are experiencing the unboxing alongside him.

Monetization Methods- Sponsored Content, Affiliate Marketing, and YouTube Ads

Unbox Therapy's monetization methods mirror those of other successful tech YouTubers. Lewis earns a significant portion of his income through sponsored content, where brands pay him to feature their products. In addition, affiliate marketing plays a large role, as he often includes links to the products featured in his videos. Lastly, YouTube ad revenue supplements his income, though it's the combination of sponsorships and affiliate marketing that truly drives his profitability.

Find a Niche- Specializing in one area, such as unboxing, can help you stand out from other creators. Focusing on a niche allows you to build an audience that shares a specific interest.

Create Suspenseful, Engaging Content- Your presentation matters. Keep your audience hooked

Chapter 17

Scaling and Expanding Beyond YouTube

As a tech YouTuber, building a strong presence on YouTube is just the beginning. Once you've successfully established your channel and grown a loyal audience, the next logical step is to expand your brand beyond YouTube. In this chapter, we will explore strategies to scale your presence and revenue by leveraging other platforms, creating your own website, building an email list, and developing digital products. These tactics can help you solidify your authority in the tech niche, connect with a wider audience, and diversify your revenue streams.

Expanding to Other Platforms

While YouTube remains the king of video content, branching out to other social media platforms can significantly enhance your visibility, drive traffic back to your channel, and help you build a broader personal brand. Each platform has its unique strengths, and by strategically using them, you can reach different audience segments.

Live Streaming and Community Building

Twitch, primarily known for gaming, has increasingly become a platform where content creators from all industries, including tech, can connect with their audience in real-time. By hosting live streams on Twitch, you can create a more personal connection with your followers, answering their questions live, discussing tech topics, or even showcasing behind-the-scenes content.

Live streaming allows you to engage with your community in an interactive way that YouTube videos cannot replicate. You can host Q&A sessions, do tech unboxings, provide live commentary on industry news, or just chat with your followers about anything related to tech. Building a community on Twitch can help increase your following on YouTube, as viewers will follow you across platforms to stay up-to-date with your content.

Additionally, Twitch offers monetization opportunities through subscriptions, donations, and ads, making it an attractive platform for YouTubers looking to diversify their revenue. The unique format of live streaming on Twitch allows you to connect with your audience in real-time, further strengthening your personal brand.

Short-Form Content and Viral Potential

TikTok has become a powerhouse in content creation, especially for short-form videos. The platform's algorithm rewards creativity and virality, making it an excellent place for tech YouTubers to gain exposure, even if you're just starting out.

On TikTok, you can create quick, engaging content such as tech tips, gadget reviews, or even snippets from your YouTube videos. Because TikTok prioritizes videos that have high engagement—likes, shares, and comments—your content has the potential to go viral if it resonates with viewers. Tech content, such as "Did you know?" tech hacks or bite-sized reviews, is highly shareable on TikTok.

The platform also offers monetization through brand partnerships, sponsored content, and creator funds. For tech YouTubers, TikTok provides a chance to reach a younger, trend-driven audience that may not yet be aware of your YouTube channel. The key to success on TikTok is creating content that is both informative and fun while taking advantage of popular trends and challenges.

Visual Content and Community Engagement

Instagram is a highly visual platform, making it a perfect fit for tech YouTubers who want to share product images, behind-the-scenes shots, and snippets of their videos. Instagram's features, such as stories, posts, reels, and IGTV, offer varied ways to showcase your content and engage with your audience.

Reels, in particular, are a great way to repurpose content from your YouTube channel, allowing you to reach an audience who may prefer shorter, more digestible videos. You can post teasers for upcoming content, share quick tech tips, or offer product unboxing experiences in a visually compelling way.

Instagram also allows for direct communication with followers, whether through comments, direct messages, or interactive features like polls and Q&A sessions. This creates an opportunity to build stronger connections with your audience, increase engagement, and even promote your YouTube content, events, or merchandise. Instagram also has a robust ad system, enabling you to promote your content or run sponsored campaigns.

Creating a Blog or Website

A blog or website acts as the central hub for all your content and activities. Having a well-designed website offers several benefits, including a professional platform to showcase your portfolio, share your insights, and enhance your credibility. It also provides a place to host your content in a format that isn't confined by the rules or algorithms of social media platforms.

SEO and Content Marketing

One of the main reasons to create a blog is the ability to leverage search engine optimization (SEO) to increase organic traffic. By writing in-depth articles related to the tech products you review, the tutorials you create, or the trends in the industry, you can rank in Google search results, attracting new visitors to your website and YouTube channel. SEO-friendly blog posts can include product guides, comparisons, "how-to" tutorials, and tech news, all of which can help you establish authority in the tech space.

Additionally, a blog enables you to create evergreen content—articles that remain relevant over time and continue to attract traffic. For instance, a comprehensive guide to building a custom PC can generate traffic for years after it is posted. This long-term traffic helps keep your content visible and accessible to new viewers.

Building Your Brand with a Personal Website

A personal website provides you with a dedicated platform where you can control your branding, message, and content. It allows you to showcase your YouTube videos, social media links, and any other content you've created, all in one place. You can also use your website as an e-commerce platform for selling merchandise, digital products, or offering services like consultations.

Moreover, your website can serve as a professional portfolio, highlighting your achievements, collaborations, and sponsorships. Potential brands and partners often look for a well-maintained online presence when considering whether to work with a creator.

Building an Email List

Building an email list is one of the most effective ways to connect with your audience directly and cultivate a loyal community. With an email list, you can keep your followers informed about new content, upcoming events, product releases, or special offers, without relying on social media algorithms. Email marketing also provides a direct line to your audience, enabling you to promote your content or products without the risk of your message getting lost in the noise of social media.

Strategies for Growing Your Email List

To grow your email list, offer value in exchange for email sign-ups. This could include free downloadable resources such as e-books, guides, or access to exclusive content. For instance, if you create a comprehensive buying guide for tech products, offering it for free in exchange for an email subscription can encourage your audience to sign up.

Promoting your email list on your YouTube channel, Instagram, and other social platforms is essential to building a strong email base. Make sure to include a clear call to action (CTA) in your content, encouraging people to subscribe to your email list for updates and exclusive content.

Once you have a growing email list, you can use email marketing platforms such as Mailchimp, ConvertKit, or ActiveCampaign to send regular newsletters, product promotions, or special announcements to your subscribers.

Developing Membership Programs and Subscriptions

If you have a loyal following, consider launching a membership or subscription program. Offering exclusive content, early access to videos, or personalized consultations can incentivize your audience to support you financially on a recurring basis. Platforms like Patreon and YouTube's channel memberships allow creators to offer paid memberships, giving your community special perks in exchange for ongoing support.

Scaling and expanding beyond YouTube requires a strategic approach to building your personal brand. By branching out to platforms like Twitch, TikTok, and Instagram, creating your own website, building an email list, and developing digital products, you can diversify your audience, increase your revenue, and solidify your presence as a tech influencer. The key to success lies in leveraging each platform's strengths while maintaining the consistency and authenticity that made your YouTube channel successful in the first place. By investing in these strategies, you can take your tech brand to new heights, creating lasting connections with your audience and maximizing your potential for growth.

Chapter 18

Conclusion and Next Steps

Building a successful tech YouTube channel is not an overnight endeavor, but with determination, creativity, and strategic planning, it is entirely possible to create a channel that resonates with viewers, drives engagement, and becomes a powerful platform for both personal branding and monetization. In this concluding chapter, we'll recap the key takeaways from the journey of growing your tech YouTube channel and outline the essential next steps to ensure continued success. This chapter is designed to motivate and guide you through the crucial next phases of your YouTube career, empowering you to stay consistent, adapt to changes, and push forward toward greater achievements.

The path to building a successful tech YouTube channel is multifaceted. From creating high-quality content to optimizing your videos for search engines, every element plays an essential role in your growth. Here are the key takeaways from the previous chapters, summarizing the essential components that will help guide your journey-

Content Creation is King- The foundation of any successful YouTube channel is its content. You must focus on creating content that is informative, engaging, and valuable to your target audience. Whether it's tech tutorials, gadget reviews, or industry analyses, the key is to deliver high-quality, relevant content that solves problems or answers questions that your audience is seeking.

Consistency is Crucial- Posting videos on a regular schedule builds momentum and keeps your audience engaged. Consistency doesn't just apply to the frequency of uploads; it extends to your content style, messaging, and branding. A consistent presence on YouTube helps build trust with your viewers, leading to greater audience retention and higher subscriber growth.

Understanding Your Audience- Knowing who your audience is and what they want is central to developing content that resonates with them. The use of analytics tools, such as YouTube Studio, allows you to dive deep into the demographics, interests, and behaviors of your viewers. This understanding lets you tailor your content and marketing efforts to better serve your audience.

Thumbnails, Titles, and SEO Matter- Eye-catching thumbnails and compelling titles are essential for driving clicks on your videos. Creating visually appealing thumbnails that stand out on YouTube's search results page and pairing them with titles that spark curiosity (without being misleading) is a vital skill. SEO optimization, through effective use of keywords, descriptions, tags, and metadata, also significantly improves the discoverability of your videos.

Community Engagement- Building a loyal community around your channel is just as important as creating great content. Engaging with your audience through comments, live streams, polls, and community posts helps strengthen the relationship with your viewers. A strong, engaged community fosters word-of-mouth promotion and keeps people coming back for more.

Monetization Comes After Building Value- Monetization strategies such as the YouTube Partner Program, affiliate marketing, sponsored videos, and selling digital products are powerful ways to generate revenue from your content. However, it's essential to focus on creating value for your audience first. As your channel grows and your influence increases, monetization becomes a natural extension of your efforts.

Adaptability is Key to Long-Term Success- YouTube, like any platform, is constantly evolving. Audience behavior, algorithm changes, and new features will always impact how your content is distributed. Embracing these changes, learning from your analytics, and being willing to adapt your content and strategy is essential for long-term growth. Success on YouTube is not about following rigid rules but rather about staying flexible and continuously improving.

Collaboration and Networking- Networking with other creators, especially those within your niche, can provide valuable opportunities for growth. Collaborations allow you to tap into new audiences, share expertise, and exchange ideas. Being part of a creator community also helps you stay motivated and inspired to push forward in your journey.

With the foundational steps laid out and the strategies outlined throughout this book, the next phase in your YouTube journey is to take deliberate and consistent actions to continue growing your channel and personal brand. These next steps will help you build upon the momentum you've already established and ensure that your channel evolves and thrives in the ever-changing landscape of YouTube.

Create a Content Calendar

Consistency is essential, and the best way to maintain it is by developing a content calendar. This calendar will help you organize your ideas, schedule uploads, and ensure that you are continually delivering fresh content to your audience. Plan ahead by outlining video topics, scripting your content, and aligning your releases with any seasonal trends or upcoming product launches in the tech world.

A content calendar helps you avoid burnout and ensures that you are regularly producing and uploading videos. Additionally, planning in advance allows you to focus on quality over quantity, dedicating more time to perfecting each video before it goes live. A well-organized content calendar will also help you track performance and identify what types of content are resonating with your audience.

Optimize Your Channel

Once you've begun producing content consistently, it's time to look at the overall health of your channel. Review your YouTube channel's branding—your profile picture, banner, about section, and links—to ensure that everything aligns with your identity as a creator. It's important to have a cohesive brand that is easily recognizable and reflects the type of content you produce.

Consider optimizing your channel description with keywords that are relevant to your niche, making it easier for new viewers to discover your channel. Creating a trailer or introductory video for new subscribers is also a great way to hook potential followers right from the start. This trailer should give them an idea of what kind of content to expect and encourage them to subscribe.

Experiment with New Content Formats

While it's essential to have a signature content style, don't be afraid to experiment with new formats. YouTube has evolved beyond just long-form tutorials and reviews; creators are now exploring a variety of formats like shorts, live streams, and even podcasts.

Testing different video formats can help you reach new audiences. For example, if you traditionally create longer, in-depth tutorials, experimenting with YouTube Shorts can introduce your channel to viewers who prefer quick, snappy content. Live streams are another effective way to engage your audience in real-time, answering questions or providing commentary on tech news, trends, or product launches.

Diversify Your Revenue Streams

Once you've built a consistent and engaged audience, it's time to explore multiple revenue streams. This doesn't just mean YouTube ads; there are a variety of monetization methods to consider. Affiliate marketing, where you earn a commission from product recommendations, is a great way to supplement your income. You can also work with brands to create sponsored content, or sell your own merchandise such as branded t-shirts or tech accessories.

Developing and selling digital products like e-books or online courses is another excellent way to maximize your revenue while offering valuable content to your audience. Crowdfunding platforms like Patreon or Buy Me a Coffee can also provide recurring income and exclusive perks for your most loyal supporters.

Keep Learning and Adapting

YouTube's algorithm, audience behaviors, and trends evolve constantly, so one of the most important next steps is to keep learning and adapting. Stay up-to-date with the latest YouTube updates and best practices by following industry blogs, attending webinars, and participating in YouTube creator communities. Consistently analyzing your channel's performance data in YouTube Studio will also give you invaluable insights into what's working and what needs adjustment.

The key to continued success is being open to learning from your audience, experimenting with new ideas, and making improvements based on feedback and analytics. It's important to view challenges as learning opportunities, and not as setbacks. Overcoming obstacles is part of the process, and with each hurdle, you grow stronger as a content creator.

Stay Motivated and Persistent

Success on YouTube doesn't happen overnight. There will be challenges, both technical and emotional, and moments where you feel like giving up. However, it's crucial to remain motivated and persistent. Your journey as a tech YouTuber will have its ups and downs, but the key is to stay focused on your goals, learn from your experiences, and continue to push forward.

One of the most powerful ways to stay motivated is to remember your "why" – the reason you started your channel in the first place. Whether it's a passion for tech, the desire to educate others, or building a personal brand, keep that reason at the forefront of your mind. Celebrate your wins, big and small, and stay connected with your audience, who will continue to be your biggest supporters along the way.

Building a successful tech YouTube channel requires more than just uploading videos; it involves continuous learning, creative experimentation, and strategic planning. By creating high-quality content, engaging with your audience, and diversifying your revenue streams, you can scale your channel and turn it into a sustainable business. Remember that success on YouTube is not solely about the number of views or subscribers you have; it's about the value you provide, the community you build, and the long-term impact you make on your audience.

Stay adaptable, stay consistent, and most importantly, stay passionate about your content. The journey may be long, but the rewards—both personal and professional—are well worth the effort. Now is the time to take the knowledge you've gained from this guide and put it into action. Your tech YouTube channel's success is waiting for you—so take the next step and make it happen.

THE END

www.ingramcontent.com/pod-product-compliance
Lightning Source LLC
LaVergne TN
LVHW022344060326
832902LV00022B/4229